Rock and Roll

TORONTO

Rock and Roll TORONTO

From Alanis to Zeppelin

JOHN GODDARD
RICHARD CROUSE

Doubleday Canada Limited

Canadian Cataloguing in Publication Data

Goddard, John, 1950–   .
    Rock and roll Toronto

Includes index.
ISBN 0-385-25600-0

1. Rock music – Ontario – Toronto – History and criticism.
2. Rock music – Ontario – Toronto – Guidebooks.
3. Toronto (Ont.) – Guidebooks. I. Crouse, Richard, 1963–   .
II. Title.

ML3534.G62 1997   781.66'09713541   C96-932240-2

Cover photographs: Neil Young/Jeffrey Blake; Alanis Morissette/Matthew Kris-MacCormack; Pete Townsend/*Toronto Sun*; Barenaked Ladies/Neil Prime-Coote; El Mocambo/Kathryn Exner; Bob Dylan/Tom Robe
Cover collage by Eric Colquhoun
Cover design by Avril Orloff
Text design by Heidy Lawrance Associates
Printed and bound in the USA

Published in Canada by
Doubleday Canada Limited
105 Bond Street
Toronto, Ontario
M5B 1Y3

CONTENTS

"It's easy to form a rock-and-roll band.
All you need is three chords and the truth."

– Brendan Canning,
bassist for Toronto band hHead

INTRODUCTION

At about the time the Beatles first topped the British charts with "Please Please Me," Richard Crouse was born in Liverpool by the banks of the Mersey River. Liverpool, Nova Scotia. It's on the south coast midway between Yarmouth and Halifax. He grew up a long way from the Mersey Beat, but as a young teenager he felt a connection, eagerly tuning in to the latest radio hits and becoming a voracious consumer of music trivia. Other kids spent their allowance on movies and cigarettes; Crouse blew his on pop-music books and magazines.

"I was really indiscriminate," he says. "I bought any music press that I could lay my hands on, whether it was *Hit Parader,* or *Creem* magazine, or those cheesy little bios that would come out constantly. Someone would have one hit, and then three weeks later there would be a book on the stands about them. I used to read all those."

While still in high school, Crouse worked as a part-time disc jockey at local radio station CKBW and as host of an after-school dance show on cable television called *Get Dancin'.* He wrote an unpublished biography of the Rolling Stones, which he considered "the definitive word" on the group, and for the school newspaper he wrote a music column called "Stardust," named after David Bowie's *The Rise and Fall of Ziggy Stardust and the Spiders from Mars.*

Opportunities in Liverpool to actually hear live music were minimal, Crouse says. He got to Halifax sometimes to hear Kiss, Rush, and a few other groups, and he once heard the Stampeders play "Sweet City Woman" at the Liverpool Memorial Arena. But otherwise he was stuck listening to cover bands at high-school dances. "I knew if I wanted to follow music I had to move to Toronto," he says.

As soon as he turned 17, Crouse made the move. He arrived at the airport at around 4 p.m., dropped his luggage at his brother's apartment, and headed straight for the El Mocambo to see B.B. Gabor, "a new-wave guy from Hungary who actually did a great version of 'Big Yellow Taxi.'" From then on, he went to the El Mocambo and to clubs along Queen Street West every chance he got. He started bussing tables at a restaurant, and with his first tips bought a needed pair of slacks and a David Wilcox record. He revived his "Stardust" column in a local television guide called *TV Facts,* and later became the pop-music columnist at the *Outrider* and *Our Toronto* newspapers. He also revived his part-time broadcasting career, becoming the pop-music commentator on CBC Radio's local afternoon show *Later the Same Day.* That exposure led to national monthly appearances on CBC's *Morningside,* with Peter Gzowski, and guest appearances on such network television shows as CTV's *Dini,* with Dini Petty.

I first heard of Crouse through my youngest sister, Marj. In 1992, she flew to Nevada with Crouse to get married in the chapel where Elvis Presley marries Ann-Margret at the end of *Viva Las Vegas.* As a surprise, Marj had arranged for an Elvis impersonator to give her away. "He walked me down the aisle singing 'Love Me Tender,'" she recalls, "and Richard was so nervous he didn't realize what was happening until we got to the altar." After the ceremony, the new-lyweds flew to Los Angeles for a honeymoon at the hotel pictured on *Hotel California,* by the Eagles.

I figured out fairly quickly that Crouse was a major music fan with a special interest in rock-and-roll landmarks. I was writing for magazines in Montreal at the time, and met him at a party he and Marj threw after the wedding. We started talking music, and at one point he told me about a trip he once took to England.

"I was in London," he says, recalling the details for me again recently. "I had a number of things that I wanted to see, but in particular I wanted to go into Abbey Road Studios and actually have a look around. I couldn't find it. There are a lot of Abbey Roads – London is a lot of little villages stuck together – and nobody could give me directions. That's the thing that amazed me. I couldn't find a book on it, nor could I find anyone who could say, 'Oh, yeah, the Beatles, Abbey Road, you take the Underground to such-and such.' Then I was in the pub around the corner from the hotel where I was staying, and I was talking to somebody at the bar and they said, 'Well, it's just two blocks up.' I went up and there it was. I was on Abbey Road. Of course I got my picture taken walking across the crosswalk, and that's when it occured to me that there should be a book – a book of rock-and-roll landmarks."

This last remark became the seed for our own book, although it took a while to germinate. My background is in news reporting. I worked for years for the Canadian Press wire service in Toronto, Ottawa, Montreal, and Yellowknife – at times as a picture editor and photographer, at other times as a reporter. I liked the serious issues, the blockbuster events. In early 1981, when the American diplomatic hostages were freed after 444 days of captivity at the hands of Iranian revolutionaries, I was one of half a dozen Western correspon-dents reporting from Tehran.

Pop-music trivia was not exactly my specialty. Far from it. I once turned down a chance to invest in Trivial Pursuit. I knew the co-inventors from Montreal, and they tried to sell me the last $1,000 share to pay for the board design. Had I invested I would have been a millionaire within a year, but I backed off thinking, "Nobody's going to want to play a trivia game."

Getting to know Crouse changed my outlook. His enthusiasm for music trivia was infectious, and talking to him always got me thinking about rock music in a detailed, personal way. I recalled buying my first record – the first Rolling Stones' LP – while growing up outside Toronto in Markham. I remembered my first concert – the Stones at Maple Leaf Gardens, in 1966. Over the next several months, other memories flooded to mind of seeing the Doors, the Band, Steppenwolf, and Blood, Sweat & Tears, until finally I phoned Crouse and said, "How about writing a book together on rock-and-roll landmarks of Toronto?"

"Great idea," he said. His problem was that he was working full-time at Southern Accent, a Cajun restaurant on Markham Street. Between that job and his broadcasting assignments, he was too busy to write.

"I'll research and write it if you help point the way," I said, and the unlikely collaboration began.

Together we laid out the ground rules. The book would be a series of self-contained items. Each would start with an address, or "rock-and-roll landmark." We would be a self-appointed two-person committee charged with declaring rock-and-roll historic sites. Sometimes we began with an obvious landmark such as Maple Leaf Gardens, then looked for a story. Sometimes we started with a major hit such as "Born to Be Wild" then looked for a landmark. Sometimes we began with a fan, or a promoter, or a retailer, then matched that person to groups and landmarks – a search that lead us naturally to stadiums and bars, but also unexpectedly to a laundromat, a church, and an elevator.

We kept our criteria loose. Historical and entertainment value ranked high on the list, along with anything surprising that was not already known. We found the house where Neil Young was conceived. We met Joni Mitchell's former landlady. We discovered the truth behind the legend about a "blind angel" rescuing Keith Richards from a jail sentence. And we located the exact spot where the Toronto police ordered Madonna not to touch herself (a room within the Toronto Argonauts' dressing room at the SkyDome). But those were the big stories. Any item that might illuminate some aspect, however small, of the music industry qualified for consideration, including Ontario Premier Bob Rae's secret dream to write a hit song.

At first we defined "rock and roll" as "any music that makes you rock." We then went beyond that definition. We included nonrock artists such as Loreena McKennitt, the Celtic harpist, whose story has lessons for other independent musicians. And we included Percy Faith, the pop conductor who as a teenager performed a selfless act of heroism that might otherwise have been lost to history. By our criteria, any compelling story about a musician known to pop music became potentially eligible.

We would not try to be historians. We would not try to get everything. We would pursue the subject as rock-and-roll fans, with the aim of celebrating both the music and the city of Toronto.

Most of the people who contributed to this project appear in the text, but some do not, and they deserve special mention. Jane Finlayson and Anne Francis carefully read each item as it was written and offered invaluable guidance. Financial and various types of logistical support came from Jim Cashmore, Sylvia Cashmore, Marj Crouse, Margot Gibb-Clark, Eric Goddard, Judy Goddard, Paul Goddard, Mary Jane McIntyre, and Bob Moenck. Lesley Grant and John Neale at Doubleday were the first to express enthusiasm for the project. Kathryn Exner supervised and edited the work, offering countless thoughtful suggestions. Janine Laporte, Christine Innes, Shaun Oakey, and Gloria Goodman skillfully helped guide the project to completion.

People who helped with photo research include David Houghton, Mark Kearney, Margaret Kemper, Rick MacMillan, Tyson Parker, Elana Rabinovitch, Randy Ray, and Dan Wright.

People who helped with various types of editorial demands include Liza Algar, Edgar Cowan, Jim Cuddy, Scott Disher, John Einarson, Douglas Fetherling, Mike Filey, Teddy Fury, Maya Gallus, Wayne Grady, Gordie Johnson, Penny Kennedy, Al McMullan, Ron Macey, Andy Maize, Danny Marks, Paul Myers, Marlene Palmer, Wilder Penfield III, Merilyn Simonds, Richard Underhill, and Michael Phillip Wojewoda.

For other types of support and assistance thanks go to Greg Bannister, Louise Dessertine, Rolf Heim, Fabienne Incurvaja, Bennett Lee, Stuart McLean, Susan Phillips, Elizabeth Schaal, Dianna Symonds, Shirley Won, and Frances Wood and the gang at Southern Accent.

John Goddard, Toronto, 1997

Rock and Roll

TORONTO

From Alanis to Zeppelin

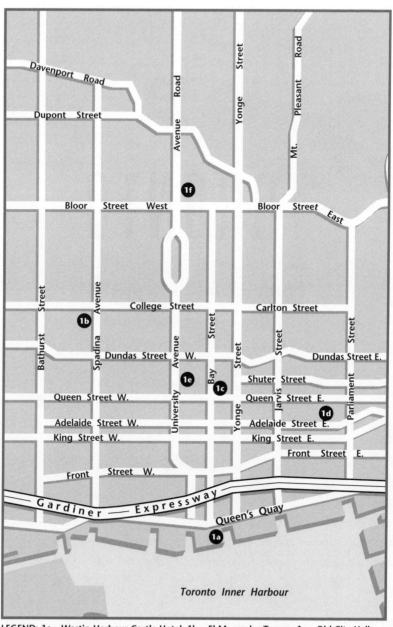

LEGEND: 1a – Westin Harbour Castle Hotel; 1b – El Mocambo Tavern; 1c – Old City Hall; 1d – Sounds Interchange; 1e – Ontario Court of Justice; 1f – Four Seasons Hotel

1

Westin Harbour Castle

1 HARBOUR SQUARE

The plan was to attract the least attention possible. On February 20, 1977, members of the Rolling Stones began to gather at the Harbour Castle Hilton – now the Westin Harbour Castle – at the lakefront where the ferries leave for the Toronto Islands. The group's contract with Atlantic Records was up for renewal, and Mick Jagger had suggested that the band strengthen its negotiating hand with a live double album. Three sides would be taken from stadium shows, particularly from an emotionally charged concert in Paris the previous year after Keith Richards's infant son, Tara, was found dead in his crib. A fourth side would be recorded at a small club in Toronto, a city handy to Atlantic's New York offices. The event would be a throwback to the band's early days. With British punk rockers snapping at their heels, the Stones would show that they could still cut it at the club level with the type of early blues and rock-and-roll numbers they played when they first started. The plan was to slip quietly into town, rehearse for a week at a studio, play two surprise club dates, and disappear again before excitement over their activity got out of hand.

The first hitch came when Keith Richards failed to show. The other Stones, with an entourage that included piano player Billy Preston and percussionist Ollie Brown, were safely ensconced on floors 29 through 34 of the hotel. Richards had yet to board a flight from England. Phone calls and telegrams to him went unanswered, but finally, on February 24, he left London with his companion, Anita Pallenberg, and son, Marlon.

The second hitch came when Richards absently tossed a blackened spoon into Pallenberg's handbag after shooting up in the airplane washroom. Toronto customs inspectors found it, along with a small amount of hashish in the same bag, and Pallenberg was arrested. She was subsequently released on a promise to appear in court.

The third hitch came four days later on Monday, February 28. Fifteen federal and provincial police officers arrived at the Harbour Castle with a warrant to search the couple's room. Richards and Pallenberg had registered in six rooms under the name Redlands, a double ruse to avoid surprises, but after 45 minutes the police found their door. Pallenberg opened it, and after several more minutes, the police found five grams of cocaine and nearly an ounce of heroin. The hard part was waking up Richards. Officers spent so much time patting his face that his cheeks turned "rosy," he later told Victor Bockris, author of *Keith Richards: The Biography*.

"What disappointed me," Richards also recalled, "was that none of them was wearing a proper Mountie's uniform. They were all in anoraks with droopy moustaches and bald heads. Real weeds, the whole lot of them, all just after their picture in the paper. Fifteen of 'em around my bed, trying to wake me up. I'd have woken up a lot quicker if I'd seen the red tunic and Smokey Bear hat."

The police drove the couple to Brampton, near the airport where the original bust had taken place. They charged Pallenberg with possession of 10 grams of high-quality hashish and a trace of heroin from the spoon, then released her on her own recognizance. They charged Richards with possession of one ounce of high-quality heroin with intent to traffic. Richards told them he had intended the drug for his own use, but the police said the trafficking charge applied because of the quantity involved. An ounce of heroin could keep the most serious junkie going for five to six weeks, they would later testify in court, estimating the street value of the seizure at $4,000. The officers postponed laying a cocaine charge pending laboratory analysis. They freed Richards on a $1,000 bond with orders to appear in court the following week.

"This may be the end of the Stones as we know them," wrote Chet Flippo in *Rolling Stone* magazine, recognizing the gravity of the bust. Only six weeks earlier, Richards had been convicted and fined in England for cocaine possession, and told that his next offence there would bring imprisonment. In Canada, trafficking carried a possible life sentence. Even if he beat a jail term, Richards could be deported on conviction and carry a criminal record that could bar him from touring anywhere in North America indefinitely, a prospect that suddenly complicated talks with Atlantic.

On Friday, March 4, Margaret Trudeau entered the picture. Over breakfast in Ottawa she and her husband, Prime Minister Pierre Trudeau, agreed privately to a 90-day trial separation. He was 56 years old; she was 27. March 4 was their sixth wedding anniversary, which neither felt like celebrating. Margaret had grown weary of the role of prime minister's wife and in recent weeks had begun publicly to rebel. At a state banquet in Venezuela she had sung a song to the president's wife, and at a formal White House dinner she had flouted protocol by wearing a calf-length dress instead of a floor-length one. Asked why by a reporter, she replied, "It's nobody's business but my own."

Now she was preparing to leave for New York, where she planned to visit friends and explore career possibilities. She had been studying photography and wished to become a photojournalist, she says in her autobiography, *Beyond Reason*. As she was packing, a woman friend called from Toronto and said, "How about dinner with the Rolling Stones?"

"Why not?" Trudeau replied. "I've just left Pierre."

The friend picked Trudeau up at the airport and drove her to the Harbour Castle Hilton, where she checked into room 2214. The two ate dinner that evening with the band members, and afterwards rode with Mick Jagger in a limousine to the El Mocambo Tavern, at 464 Spadina

(Photo: Margaret Trudeau)

Mick Jagger, in a photo taken by Margaret Trudeau, performs at the El Mocambo Tavern on March 5, 1977. "Jagger in a little green and white striped jump suit open to the point where his pubic hair presumably begins, puts on the most defiant, cocksure, strutting performance I have ever seen," wrote Chet Flippo in *Rolling Stone*.

Avenue, a rundown club with a neon sign shaped like a palm tree. Reporters spotted Trudeau and Jagger entering at the back door. Police were everywhere, and buses were arriving from CHUM radio station with 300 contest winners. April Wine, a Montreal band, played the opening set. For the next 45 minutes the stage stood empty. Then suddenly the Stones appeared and laid into the opening bars of "Route 66."

(Photo: Margaret Trudeau)

"Everybody went nuts, including me," April Wine's drummer, Jerry Mercer, still recalls. "Everybody was up on tables and chairs, yelling and screaming. Margaret Trudeau was there. She and I ended up standing on a table together."

Keith Richards (left) and Ron Wood tune together backstage in a previously unpublished photo by Margaret Trudeau, then wife of Pierre Trudeau, the Canadian prime minister. She received exclusive backstage access as a freelance press photographer.

"The Stones," wrote Chet Flippo in *Rolling Stone,* "are magnificent. Sitting five feet away from them when they are at full power is nothing short of awesome. Billy Preston slides in behind his keyboards, Ollie Brown takes up his percussion instruments behind Charlie Watts, Bill Wyman is diffidently off at the right end of the tiny stage, and Jagger is flanked by Keith and Ronnie Wood. Keith, who is gaunt and unshaven, but occasionally smiling, leads them in with 'Honky Tonk Women,' and Jagger in a little green and white

The Stones fill a tiny stage bearing the El Mocambo's trademark palm tree. "Jagger is flanked by Keith and Ronnie Wood," wrote Chet Flippo in *Rolling Stone.* "Keith (right) ... is gaunt and unshaven, but occasionally smiling."

(Photo: Margaret Trudeau)

striped jump suit open to the point where his pubic hair presumably begins, puts on the most defiant, cocksure, strutting performance I have ever seen. The members sign autographs in between numbers and at one point Jagger ends up on his back with a female admirer lying on top of him, kissing and feeling."

"Are you feeling good?" Jagger asks the crowd at one point between songs in a line heard on the finished live double album, *Love You Live.* "Are you feeling loose now? A little more relaxed?" Later he says, "Everything all right in the critics' section? Got plenty to drink, have you?" And Ron Wood adds, "Hello, Margaret, all right?"

The album includes four songs from the El Mocambo sessions: "Mannish Boy" by Muddy Waters, "Crackin' Up" by Ellas McDaniel, "Little Red Rooster" by Willie Dixon, and "Around and Around" by Chuck Berry. Two other songs on the album were also recorded in Toronto, both during a concert at Maple Leaf Gardens on June 17, 1975. One is "Fingerprint File." The other is "It's Only Rock 'n' Roll," in which Jagger changes a line to sing, "I bet you think you're the only girl in Toronto."

On Saturday, March 5, Margaret Trudeau was about to leave for New York when Ron Wood spotted her.

"Hey, where are you off to?" he asked. "Aren't you coming to tonight's session?"

"I'm not a groupie," she replied, as she recounts the exchange in her book. "I can't possibly."

"Why don't you work, then? Take some photographs."

She stayed and worked the first assignment of her intended new career, later selling a picture of Mick Jagger to *People* magazine.

The next day was Sunday. Still Trudeau stayed. She went to dinner that night with Ron Wood and Charlie Watts. At around midnight they dropped her at the hotel, saying they were going to the studio. "At 5 a.m.," she writes, "I got a call from the lobby: 'It's us. We're back. Can we come up?'" And within minutes the wife of the Canadian prime minister was letting the Rolling Stones into her hotel room.

"The whole group clattered into my room, in high spirits and drunk with the euphoria that comes from an all-night working session," she writes. "One rang down to room service for some champagne and orange juice, and another played the guitar ... We settled down to drink, play dice, smoke a little

(Photo: Kathryn Exner)

A neon sign shaped like a palm tree announces the landmark El Mocambo Tavern at 464 Spadina Avenue.

hash. Mick and Keith disappeared into a corner to work out a new number. It was fun; I was happy to be part of it. At nine o'clock we drew back the curtains on a cold grey morning and ordered coffee. One by one the Stones departed to their own rooms to sleep. Ronnie was the last to leave."

It was now Monday, March 7. Trudeau stayed another night. On Tuesday she left for New York, as did Jagger and Wood, all on separate flights. On Wednesday a whiff of scandal hit the press. Until then, news outlets had given splashy coverage to Trudeau's arrival with Jagger at the El Mocambo, and to her appearance at the club over two nights, but no reporter had connected her to the Harbour Castle. Now a rumor was circulating of a love affair between Trudeau and Jagger, and reporters – unaware of Trudeau's prior plans for New York – were viewing the flights with heightened interest.

"Premier's Wife in Stones Scandal," ran the front-page headline of the London *Daily Mirror*, suggesting that Trudeau had run off with the band. "Stones Are Cast at Mrs. Trudeau," said the New York *Daily News*.

Jagger dismissed the gossip angrily. "I'm fed up about all this talk about me and Margaret Trudeau," he told the *Toronto Star* by phone from the Manhattan apartment he shared with his wife, Bianca. "It's ridiculous. I came to Canada to do an album. That's all. And all people talk about is that I've eloped with Mrs. Trudeau. It's not just ridiculous, it's libellous." Speaking to a London newspaper, he said, "She's a bit naughty and I suppose that's a bit different in Australia, I mean Canada – they're all the same. They have nothing more to talk about really so they all start to blow things up."

Trudeau responded coyly at first. "I am very fond of him," she said of Jagger. "I like to think of him as a friend. But I hardly know him. After all, I'm a married lady." The next day she issued a curiously sweeping denial. "I'm not involved with any of them," she said.

In the public mind, the idea of an affair somehow endures. When Trudeau's book came out, some readers interpreted the line "Ronnie was the last to leave" as her way of setting the record straight.

In 1979, a former roadie for Keith Richards named Tony Sanchez said he knew the truth. "Ronnie Wood enjoyed a romantic interlude with Margaret Trudeau," he wrote in his book *Up and Down with the Rolling Stones.* "The press got everything wrong and led the world into believing that Mrs. Trudeau's fling was with Mick Jagger."

Asked about the passage today, the former Mrs. Trudeau says, "Well, I never said I had a romantic liaison with Mick Jagger."

But did she have one with Ron Wood?

"Not really, no," she says. "I wouldn't call it a romantic liaison. He was a sweetie pie. He was a nice man. But no, no. I didn't have an affair with him or anything."

Trudeau says her encounter with the Stones was significant to her for other reasons. "It was a turning point for me," she says. "It was part of leaving the prison world of 24 Sussex, living under police guard and the whole thing. To go to a Rolling Stones concert was the epitome to me of personal freedom. It was my music, my age, everything, and I had been for quite a long time living outside of my own generation as Pierre's wife. I was 27 and for the first time back with my generation – trouble that we may be."

Two and a half months later, on May 27, 1977, the Trudeaus formally separated.

Five hours after leaving the party in Margaret Trudeau's room on March 7, Keith Richards arrived by station wagon at Old City Hall, an ornately carved sandstone building at 60 Queen Street West, remodelled as a provincial courthouse. He wore a black velvet suit and a white scarf that fluttered behind him as he mounted the front steps past a small crush of cheering fans. At the top of the stairs he turned right and walked to the end of the hall to courtroom 26, since renumbered 116. There his formal arraignment took place. Richards stood in the prisoner's dock, hands folded before him, as the judge read the charge of heroin possession with intent to traffic. Richards was not required to speak. The next day in the same room, a second charge of cocaine possession was added, and bail was increased from a $1,000 bond to $25,000 cash. The judge then ordered Richards to return the following week to set a trial date.

Richards spent most of his time holed up at the hotel, but one night he went into a studio, Sounds Interchange, at 506 Adelaide Street East (now Dome Audio Visual Effects at 49 Ontario Street), where he recorded five sad songs with Ian Stewart, the piano player and original band member sometimes referred to as "the sixth Stone." They recorded "Worried Life Blues," "Say It's Not You," "Apartment No. 9," "She Still Comes Around," and "Sing Me Back Home." None of the songs was ever released, but biographer Bockris, who has heard them, says Richards sang with the "keenly expressive, edge-of-tears sound of a man straining to give vent to his emotions."

When the week was up, Richards returned to courtroom 26. The judge ordered a preliminary hearing for the end of June, the start of a long series of procedures, some of which Richards attended, some of which he skipped. The same day in suburban Brampton, Pallenberg

was convicted and fined $400. In New York, the other Stones signed
a new contract with Atlantic.

Chet Flippo of *Rolling Stone* magazine interviewed Richards at
his hotel late that day, catching a rare glimpse of the Stones guitarist
at one of the most critical points of his life and career. When asked
about the club sessions, Richards speaks happily. "It has been a
long time since I've had my legs stroked while playing," he says. "I'd
forgotten about that." When asked about his problems with authorities, however, Richards sounds bitter, even paranoid.

"I can't believe that a government would spend two seconds of
its time worrying about what rock-and-roll band is coming to its
country," he says. "But they do ... The idea is: 'Let's grab *him.*' So
it just becomes political outlaws – there really isn't any way for anybody in our position or my position to get a fair trial, because of the
image, or the prejudice, anything, anyway. It's already against me
just because of the image ... *illegal,* they are really out to make rock
and roll *illegal.*

"Really, it would be illegal to play the goddamn music," Richards
continues. "That's the basic drive behind that whole thing. They
are just scared of that rhythm. Certainly every sound has an effect
on the body and the effects of a good backbeat make these people
shiver in their boots, so you are fighting some primeval fear that
you can't even rationalize, because it's to do with the chromosomes
and the exploding genes."

Keith Richards went on trial on October 23, 1978. The proceedings
took place at the Ontario Court of Justice, at 361 University Avenue.
The morning was wet and cold. Few fans lined the sidewalk outside,
but upstairs, on the second floor, 80 young people packed courtroom

2–5 to capacity. Another couple of dozen lined the hallway, some wearing Rolling Stones T-shirts. Richards entered under police escort wearing a three-piece beige suit with a white shirt, a dark-brown flowered tie, and a gold earring in his left ear.

Mr. Justice Lloyd Graburn presided. He was a 52-year-old lover of classical music and jazz, who would say later that until taking the case, he had never heard of the Rolling Stones. The Stones themselves remained as popular as ever. After *Love You Live*, they had released a new album, *Some Girls,* and had toured the United States on the strength of it all summer. "I'm gonna find my way to heaven 'cause I did my time in hell," Richards sings on one track of his attempts at rehabilitation. "I wasn't looking too good, but I was feeling pretty well."

From the outset, it was clear that the lawyers had struck a deal. Crown prosecutor Paul Kennedy reduced the charges against Richards to one count of heroin possession. He accepted that the guitarist had intended the drug for his own use, he said, and dropped the cocaine charge for lack of proper documentation. Heroin possession, however, carried a jail term of up to seven years. Kennedy was pushing for six to twelve months.

When Richards pleaded guilty, the lawyers turned their attention to sentencing. Kennedy cited the quantity involved – one ounce of heroin, 32 percent pure (compared to the usual 10 to 20 percent). People had been jailed on smaller quantities, he said. He also cited Richards's previous convictions, emphasizing that Richards was not a teenage experimenter but an adult who understood the gravity of the offence.

Throughout the proceedings, Richards said nothing. At times he rested his head in his hands. At other times he leaned back and passed a hand through his tousled hair.

His lawyer, Austin Cooper, compared the guitarist to Judy Garland, Dylan Thomas, F. Scott Fitzgerald, and Billie Holiday. "Keith Richards," Cooper said, "is an intensely creative person who is often wracked with emotional pain. He had a poor self-image, problems with other people. His everyday life can be hell."

Cooper went on to outline Richards's history of drug addiction. He told how Richards began experimenting with drugs in 1967 after a gruelling tour that left him exhausted. "In 1969, he started with heroin and it got to the state where he was taking such quantities of the drug and getting no euphoria from it," the lawyer said. "He was taking such powerful amounts – as much as $2\frac{1}{2}$ grams a day – just to feel normal." Three times Richards had tried to kick the addiction through medical cures, and three times he had failed, the lawyer said. The current attempt, he said citing medical reports, appeared to be succeeding.

"He should not be dealt with as a special person," Cooper said, "but I ask Your Honor to understand him as a creative, tortured person – as a major contributor to an art form. He turned to heroin to prop up a sagging existence. I ask you to understand the whole man." Richards, Cooper also said, "has fought a tremendous personal battle to rid himself of this terrible problem."

At 10 a.m. the next day, the court reconvened for sentencing. Again the room was packed. The hallway crowd grew to 100 people. Mr. Justice Graburn announced his verdict: a one-year suspended sentence. "As part of your sentence," Graburn told Richards, "I am attaching a special section that during the next six months you will give a special performance … for blind people. You can put on this performance on your own or with other people of your choosing." Graburn also ordered Richards to continue a rehabilitation program in New York and to report to a Toronto probation officer twice in the coming year.

"Keith Richards's efforts have been moving him away from the drug culture," the judge said, "and this can only encourage those who emulate him. Because of all these facts, no jail or fine is appropriate."

Detractors said that the concert should be for the deaf, not the blind, and the Crown tried unsuccessfully to appeal, but the following spring Richards would fulfill his obligations by playing, with the other Stones, a concert for the blind at the Civic Auditorium in nearby Oshawa. At a news conference after the verdict, at the Four Seasons Hotel, 21 Avenue Road, Richards looked tired but relieved, answering every question in good humor.

Asked about his addiction, he said, "It's easier to get on it than get off it." Asked about reaction from the other Stones, he said, "They're pissed off I was not put away for a couple of years." Asked about his feelings for Canada, he said, "It's nothing to do with Canada, what happened. We are not going to sit down and blame it on Canadians, it could have happened anywhere. Mind you, you should do something about those Mounties." Years later on a return visit to promote his solo album, *Main Offender,* he said, "Toronto did the coolest thing by me. That straightened me up, man, the whole thing. That was when I realized that this had gone too far as an experiment."

One question remains: Why a concert for the blind? Mr. Justice Graburn is no longer living, but his youngest son, Peter, a lawyer in Calgary, says he knows the answer. Until now he has never told his story publicly, and his version differs sharply from the poetic one Keith Richards often tells about a "blind angel" coming to his rescue. "What was the reason for the decision?" Peter Graburn asks rhetorically. "It was not a blind angel."

Graburn reviews the case step by step. Once Richards pleaded guilty, a jail term had to be considered. "My father was a real stickler for the law," Graburn says. "He would rarely break ground or go against established case precedent, and there was a clear precedent for not sending a person charged with this offence to jail." The current case was more sensational than most, he says, but the judge wanted to treat Richards like anybody else.

"So he was not going to jail," Graburn says. "The alternative was a suspended sentence, and my father really pushed the idea of community service as part of a sentence. That was important to him in most decisions. If the accused was a proper candidate for it, my father was interested in having them do community service as much as possible."

Ideas were tossed around. Working with cancer patients at the Princess Margaret Hospital was proposed, then rejected for security reasons. Next door to the hospital stood the Canadian National Institute for the Blind. The Graburns had a friend in administration there. "That's how the CNIB popped to mind," Peter Graburn says. "The suggestion was more of a one-on-one, hands-on workshop idea of teaching kids or young people music. But practicalities came into play, and the workshops ended up being a concert."

The "blind angel" legend grew from a small human-interest story published the day after the verdict in the *Toronto Sun*. It told of a 24-year-old blind woman from Montreal, Rita Bedard, who claimed to have planted the idea of a concert for the blind with Richards's lawyer, Austin Cooper. The paper also quoted Cooper telling a reporter, "That's just not true. It was as much a surprise to me as it was to you."

The article described Bedard as a "superfan" who had been to Stones concerts in Buffalo, Detroit, Chicago, Anaheim, Philadelphia, and elsewhere. On a bus once to New York her money was stolen, the paper quotes her as saying, and when the group heard about it they gave her $100.

"The whole group has been giving me the strength to carry on," she said. "The only thing I had left ... was music. I'm so proud that Keith could do something for the blind. I'll have to move to Toronto now to be closer to Keith. He's going to be here."

Bedard never claimed to have spoken to the judge directly. The paper said only that after getting Richards's autograph and a peck on the cheek from him, she kissed her "Free Keef" button and declared, "You're free, my darling, I told you I'd get you free."

In Richards's mind, details of the story somehow transformed themselves over time. In 1989, he was asked his version of events in the television documentary *25x5,* now available on home video.

"And then the blind angel comes into the picture," he says on the tape. "This little chick from Toronto, she's totally blind. There is nothing would stop this girl from turning up at gigs. So I'd fix her up. 'Hey, give the girl a ride, man.' You know, I had visions of her being run over and God knows what can happen to a blind chick on the road. This chick went to the judge's house in Toronto, personally, and she told him this simple story, you know. And I think from there he figured out the way to get Canada and himself and myself out of the hook. And so he sentenced me to a concert for the blind, which I gladly performed, you know, and my blind angel came through, bless her heart."

"Absolutely not, no way," says Peter Graburn, but the story is now a fixture in Stones lore. To many fans, the idea that a blind angel came to Richards's rescue further testifies to his invincibility and to the Stones' reputation for being above the law. They could roll into town, mess with the prime minister's wife, get busted for heroin trafficking, and instead of being banned from the country forever, get invited by a judge to play a concert.

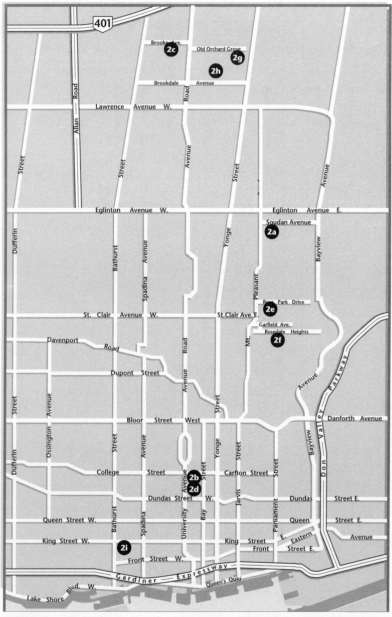

LEGEND: 2a – 361 Soudan Avenue; 2b – Toronto General Hospital; 2c – 315 Brooke Avenue; 2d – Hospital for Sick Children; 2e – 133 Rose Park Drive; 2f – Whitney Public School; 2g – 49 Old Orchard Grove; 2h – John Wanless Public School; 2i – Ciccone's Dining Lounge

2
Neil Young
Sightseeing Tour

361 SOUDAN AVENUE

A small two-storey house of dark-red brick in north Toronto is the site of Neil Young's conception – on the dining-room floor during a record snowfall on February 4, 1945.

"I know the exact time," his father, Scott, recalls in *Neil and Me,* a memoir published in 1984. "I remember the street in Toronto, the wild February blizzard through which only the hardiest moved, on skis, sliding downtown through otherwise empty streets to otherwise empty offices. All trains were marooned or cancelled."

Scott would later become a journalist and novelist, popular especially among successive waves of Canadian boys for his hockey books: *Scrubs on Skates* (1952), *Boy on Defence* (1953), and *Boy at the Leafs' Camp* (1962). At the time, he was a sub-lieutenant in the Navy on home leave. He, his wife, Rassy, and their 3-year-old son, Bob, were spending the day at the home of Ian and Lola Munro,

(Photo: John Goddard)

A two-storey house of dark-red brick stands at 361 Soudan Avenue, where Neil Young was conceived during a record snowfall on February 4, 1945. "I know the exact time," says his father, Scott.

at 361 Soudan Avenue near Eglinton Avenue and Mount Pleasant Road, when the storm hit.

Newspapers from the time show that five inches of snow fell that evening, bringing the total since November to 63.4 inches, or more than five feet – more than normally fell in an entire winter. "This makes a new record for concentrated snowfall," Harold Bradley, the street-cleaning commissioner, told reporters at the time. After dinner, the Youngs had no choice but to stay over.

"A mattress was hauled down to the dining-room floor and shoved against the wall for Rassy and me," Scott writes. "We were just past our middle twenties and had been apart for most of the previous year … We were healthy young people, much in love … We tried to be fairly quiet."

TORONTO GENERAL HOSPITAL, 585 University Avenue

On November 12, 1945, at about 8 a.m., Neil entered the world at what was then called the Private Patients' Pavilion of Toronto General Hospital, since renamed the Thomas J. Bell Wing. It is a lofty, brown-brick structure built in 1930, with a functioning grandfather clock in the lobby and chairs old enough to have been in place the day Neil was born.

"He had a lot of black hair," Scott recalls of his first glimpse of the boy.

315 BROOKE AVENUE

A modest three-bedroom bungalow became the Youngs' first home. It was numbered 335 then, north of Lawrence Avenue and west of Avenue Road. Now the site supports a monster home, but on most neighboring lots stand the original 1940s bungalows that Neil must have known as a toddler.

The war was over. Scott was working as an assistant editor at *Maclean's* magazine, making $4,000 a year. Money was tight. To supplement his salary, he began to write short stories in his spare time. Bob and Neil shared a bedroom, and in the extra one Scott wrote at a roll-top desk for two hours every Tuesday and Thursday evening, and every Saturday and Sunday morning. Rassy typed and mailed the stories, and over the next three years sales to such magazines as *Collier's, Women's Home Companion,* and *Saturday Evening Post* cleared the family of its most pressing debts.

Neil displayed an early musical affinity. "In his playpen, when the record player or radio was on, he would jig to Dixieland music even before he could stand up by himself," Scott recalls. "His whole body moved to the rhythm."

THE HOSPITAL FOR SICK CHILDREN, 555 University Avenue

The first hospital in North America dedicated to caring for children moved from 67 College Street to its current location on University

Avenue in 1949. Two years later, Scott and Rassy rushed there with 5-year-old Neil, fearing for his life.

By then, they were living 70 miles northeast of Toronto in Omemee, a village of 750 people. They had sold the Brooke Avenue house in early 1948, when Neil was 2½ and when Scott quit *Maclean's* to write fiction full time. Late one night, Scott heard Neil groan painfully in his bed and got up to investigate.

"What's the matter, pally?" he asked his son.

"My back hurts," the boy replied.

By the next morning, Neil could barely move his neck, and he screamed when anybody touched his head. Scott and Rassy feared the worst. A polio epidemic had been raging all summer, attacking mostly children – sometimes killing within hours, sometimes crippling for life.

That afternoon, the whole family drove through a lightning storm to the hospital, where a doctor drained a sample of Neil's spinal fluid for testing. "The test is positive," said the doctor 15 minutes later. "That means he has the disease."

For the next several days on the isolation ward, Neil endured excruciating pain. He would try to sit upright to relieve his back, clinging to the sides of his cot. When he dozed off he would fall backwards again, waking in agony. After seven days, however, the worst of the symptoms had passed.

"I didn't die, did I?" Scott remembers the boy saying.

Neil had survived, but a resulting weakness on his left side was to bring terrible back problems in adulthood. "I was in and out of hospitals for the two years between *After the Gold Rush* [1970] and *Harvest* [1972]," he later told *Rolling Stone* magazine. "I have one weak side and all the muscles slipped on me. My discs slipped. I couldn't hold my guitar up … I wore a brace … I could only stand up four hours a day … The doctors were starting to talk about wheelchairs, so I had some discs removed."

133 ROSE PARK DRIVE

In the summer of 1954, when Neil was eight, the Youngs moved to their most distinguished address yet, a handsome red-brick duplex on a quiet street in Toronto's Moore Park district, near St. Clair Avenue and Mount Pleasant Road. The boys enrolled at nearby Whitney Public School.

The family moved there because of domestic problems. While still in Omemee, Scott had begun to take out-of-town news assignments for *Sports Illustrated.* On one trip, he "fell for a woman," as he puts it. He felt torn. On his next trip he wrote Rassy asking for a divorce. He mailed the letter, then changed his mind. He pleaded for forgiveness. Rassy took him back. They made plans. Instead of going to Florida for the winter as previously arranged, they took the duplex on Rose Park Drive.

"It was a terrible time," Scott recalls. "The year was full of tears and recriminations and reunions and separations again. I simply don't know what the effect on Bob and Neil was of this going away and then coming back to say, Look, I'm home now, I love you – only to go away again."

That winter Scott wrote his first novel, *The Flood.* "And then the flood came," the jacket copy reads. "Martin was to find solace not in his children, but in the person of a married woman."

BROCK ROAD, PICKERING

The place has since burned down, and never did have a street number, but in 1955 a frame bungalow on two acres of property 30 miles east of Toronto in Pickering offered sanctuary to the Youngs in their search for calm. "We made a new start," Scott writes. He dropped fiction writing again to take a public-relations job with a jet-engine manufacturer, Orenda Engines. A year later, he switched to become a daily columnist at the country's most prestigious newspaper, the Toronto *Globe and Mail.*

Neil made the most of his surroundings. In July 1956, when he was 10, he acquired 30 fertilized eggs, which he hatched into chickens. Every morning before breakfast he would feed and water them, and set them loose from an old coop in a back field. By the second summer, with more chickens, he was clearing $20 a week in egg sales.

"Maybe you can imagine the thrill of watching young chicks grow into healthy, husky chickens," he wrote in a school composition that Scott quotes. "When I finish school I plan to go to Ontario Agricultural College."

49 OLD ORCHARD GROVE

A few blocks from Neil's first address on Brooke Avenue stands a tidy two-storey brick structure with a front bay window. In late 1958, when Neil was 13, the Youngs bought the house and moved back from Pickering so that Scott could be closer to work. By then he was one of Canada's best-known journalists. He was writing a daily sports column for the *Globe and Mail* and appearing as intermission host on the country's most popular television show, *Hockey Night in Canada.*

Neil took a job as a paper boy, and enrolled in Grade 7 at John Wanless Public School, at nearby 250 Brookdale Avenue. He was also getting into music. Late at night, he would listen to the local Top 40 radio station CHUM 1050 and to other stations picked up from the southern United States. "That's when I really became aware of what was going on," he once told rock journalist Cameron Crowe. "I knew that I wanted to play, that I was into it. 'Maybe,' by the

Chantels, 'Short Fat Fannie,' Elvis Presley, Larry Williams, Chuck Berry, those were the first people I heard. I used to just fall asleep listening to music. I was a real swinger."

He began to play his first instrument, a plastic ukulele. "The first thing I learned is that three chords are the basis to a lot of songs," he told British rock journalist Nick Kent, as quoted in Kent's 1994 essay collection, *The Dark Stuff.*

In late 1958, the Youngs moved to 49 Old Orchard Grove where Neil, at the age of 13, began to play a plastic ukulele. "I basically just taught myself," he says. *(Photo: John Goddard)*

"It's a blues-based idea. You start in G, go to C, and resolve it all with a D chord. So I learnt how to work those three chords and then got into the thing of working in different keys. I basically just taught myself, figuring out as I went along."

CICCONE'S DINING LOUNGE, 601 King Street West

"Down on Pain Street disappointment lurks," Neil sings in "Time Fades Away." More specifically it lurked on King Street, east of Bathurst, in the shadowy corners of Ciccone's Dining Lounge.

The restaurant was founded in 1943 by Frank and Mary Ciccone. From the outside it looks ordinary – a flat concrete wall painted in green, pink, and yellow pastels, with yellow awnings over a row of tiny windows. Inside, a set of low archways creates an atmosphere that must have seemed exotic once, each table covered with a gingham cloth and lit by a candle. Frank Ciccone died years ago, but Mary still presides over the business and waits on tables. "I've known Neil since he was in the oven," she says with her unrestrained laugh.

The Youngs often ate at Ciccone's as a family, and it was to Ciccone's that Scott took his sons one evening in September 1959 to say that he was leaving them for good this time. Bob was 17, Neil not yet 14. During an assignment out west for the *Globe and Mail,* Scott had fallen in love with a press officer named Astrid Mead.

"I tried to explain to them that I loved them but that I didn't want to live with their mother any more," Scott writes in *Neil and Me.* "I'm not sure I made much sense. After dinner, the three of us walked back east along King Street to where the *Globe and Mail* building was then, at King and York. When we parted there, Neil reached over and patted me on the shoulder as if he was sorry for me." The following year, Rassy and the boys moved to Winnipeg.

"Helpless, helpless, helpless," Neil sings in his 1970 childhood reminiscence, "Helpless," with Crosby, Stills, Nash and Young.

"His music always had a sort of forlorn

(Photo: John Goddard)

"Down on Pain Street disappointment lurks," sings Neil Young in "Time Fades Away." Pain and disappointment also lurked for him at Ciccone's Dining Lounge, near King and Bathurst Streets, in September 1959.

and desolate undertone," Rassy once said. "At times I would wonder why his face would light up with a sort of joy when he'd play something he'd composed that was so sad it brought tears to my eyes."

(Photo: Jeffrey Bloke)

One of rock's greatest and most enduring performers, Neil Young takes the stage at Copps Coliseum in Hamilton, Ontario during his Smell the Horse tour in 1991. "I knew that I wanted to play and that I was into it," he recalls of his early Toronto days.

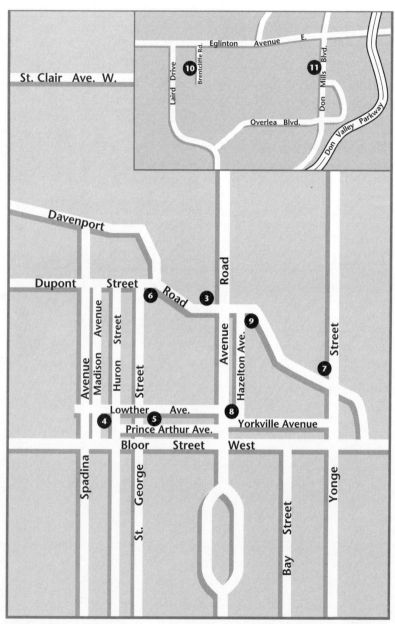

LEGEND: 3 – Brave New World; 4 – 504 Huron Street; 5 – The Sparrows' Nest; 6 – Wash and Dry Self-Serve Laundry; 7 – The Concert Hall; 8 – The Purple Onion; 9 – Nimbus 9 Productions; 10 – *RPM Weekly*; 11 – Ontario Science Centre

3

Brave New World

The building resembles a small warehouse, two storeys high, set back behind a parking lot near the intersection of Davenport and Avenue Roads. "Hazelton House," says the sign outside. "Exclusive fabrics and decorations to the trade." The building now serves as a cloth wholesaler to furniture and drapery manufacturers, but for a brief period in the early 1960s, the upstairs functioned as an after-hours club called Brave New World.

Its star attraction was David Clayton-Thomas. He was a burly, big-voiced white rhythm-and-blues singer who, as leader of the house band, was beginning to experiment with various combinations of musical styles and forms. "I use the word 'rock' almost as a disparaging term," he once said, meaning that he longed to expand on early rock and roll to create a richer, more sophisticated sound.

At Brave New World, he exchanged ideas with a wide variety of musicians who dropped by informally to play. He made connections there that led to his pioneering efforts at fusing a rock backbeat to chord structures and orchestrations borrowed from jazz and classical music, efforts that in turn led him to New York and stardom. In 1969, Clayton-Thomas became lead singer and front man for Blood, Sweat & Tears, the band most responsible for launching jazz-rock as a dominant musical style in the early 1970s. "Even the Rolling Stones started taking horns on the road," he recalls.

Clayton-Thomas sometimes describes himself as a jailhouse kid made good. He was born in 1941 in England to a Canadian serviceman and an English music-hall entertainer, and moved with them when he was six to the Toronto suburb of Willowdale. "My father didn't understand me at all, but then neither did I," he once said. He grew up restless and rebellious. He smoked cigarettes, stole doughnuts, and wore a black leather jacket with zippers, like Marlon Brando in *The Wild One*. He and his friends, he recalls, "used to park our bicycles down the street and walk to restaurants so people would think we had motorcycles." By the time he was 15, he was sleeping in parked cars and in office buildings. Then he went to jail.

"I spent from age 15 to 21 as a guest of the Canadian government," he says, meaning that he spent more than four years incarcerated at various reformatories and institutions for crimes that began with swiping a car in Hull, Quebec, and later involved punching a cop. "Burwash Industrial Farm, Guelph Reformatory, Millbrook maximum security – I guess that's when I really started to attach myself to the blues. I hung out with a lot of black kids who exposed me to John Lee Hooker and Lightnin' Hopkins. I adore that music to this day. I became aware of Motown and R&B, everything from Bobby 'Blue' Bland to Ray Charles to Aretha Franklin."

At Burwash, he also started singing at special events. He didn't have a guitar, but another inmate did, and Clayton-Thomas learned to play by drawing frets and strings on a cribbage board and singing notes as he pretended to pick.

"I knew what the notes were, and I have excellent pitch," he says. "Always have had. The horn section of Blood, Sweat & Tears could tune to my voice. If I told them that's the note – bang, that's the note."

On his release in 1962, Clayton-Thomas returned to Toronto, By day, he operated an extruder at Canada Wire and Cable, off Eglinton Avenue East in suburban Leaside, covering wire with polyethylene insulation. By night, he hung out at the bars on lower Yonge Street, listening to rhythm-and-blues bands and getting into fights.

"It was an angry era and I was a very angry young man," he says, but he was also determined to make something of himself through music. He discovered that blues, R&B, and soul had penetrated Yonge Street in his absence, fiery black music carried up from radio stations in Chicago and Detroit. Top acts regularly came to town as well. Bo Diddley and Muddy Waters could sometimes be seen at Le Coq d'Or, at 333 Yonge Street, now the HMV music store. The Primettes (with Diana Ross) and Little Stevie Wonder would appear at the Club Blue Note, at 372A Yonge Street, now a used CD and vinyl store called Just for the Record. Live music could also be heard at the Friar's Tavern, the Colonial, the Brown Derby, and other Yonge Street bars; some of the bands came from out of town, others from a growing local pool of talent dominated at the time by Rompin' Ronnie Hawkins, the fabled rough-and-tumble rockabilly band leader who had relocated from Arkansas in 1958. "A fighter's got to fight, a football player's got to play football, a musician's got to play in front of a crowd," Hawkins never tires of saying, "and Yonge Street was one of the greatest streets on the planet for rock and roll."

Determined to find a place in the scene, Clayton-Thomas began by studying Hawkins and his Hawks, usually at Le Coq d'Or. The group included Robbie Robertson on guitar, Levon Helm on drums, and the other players who later became famous as the Band. "Watching them made you want to do it all the more," Clayton-Thomas recalls, and with four young musicians he saw constantly at the same shows, he formed his own band featuring a hot guitar player named Freddie Keeler. Clayton-Thomas took the name Sonny Thomas, and started billing the band as Sonny Thomas and the Fabulous Shays.

From the beginning, Clayton-Thomas wanted to develop his own sound. He wanted to experiment, and soon found the bar scene too restrictive. "On Yonge Street you had to play Top 40," he recalls. "You played five shows a night, and you literally would rehearse till dawn to keep up with whatever was on the hit parade."

He found his outlet at the weekend after-hours clubs. Several existed then, mostly loft-type places downtown that opened either at 11:30 p.m. or after the bars closed at 1 a.m. He favored the Imperial Club at Yonge and Queen, and the Club Blue Note, the city's premier R&B venue, where he quickly made friends with the house musicians and often got invited up to sing.

"There was Steve Kennedy on tenor sax and Doug Riley on piano," he recalls, "and everybody from the Righteous Brothers to the Temptations, whoever happened to be in the neighborhood, would come by. We didn't get paid for it. I would come because I would get a chance to sing a duet with [local R&B singer] Dianne Brooks, or we would have King Curtis [formerly with the Coasters] sit in on saxophone, and Robbie Robertson play guitar, and Levon Helm sit in on drums. There would be three or four different drummers in the course of the night. Guys would just be walking in, sit in for two or three tunes, then somebody else would take over, and it would go on all night long."

Such nights gave him a sense, well before the Beatles, that music was about to change. "There were young guys coming out of the conservatories with a complete classical and jazz background," he says, "but who grew up with Chuck Berry and Little Richard and Fats Domino, the same music I grew up with, and it was only a matter of time before we began to express ourselves."

In early 1964, Clayton-Thomas saw a way to make late-night performing his livelihood. A new after-hours club called Brave New World had opened in upper Yorkville. The owner was Duff Roman, a well-known figure on the local pop scene. He was a disc jockey at Top 40 radio station CKEY (across the street from the club), a frequent concert emcee, and a summer dance host north of the city in the Muskoka Lakes district. He knew everybody, and opening a weekend after-hours house seemed a logical extension of his activities.

"I was the terrible person who brought rock and roll to Yorkville," Roman says jocularly now of Brave New World, the only rock club in what was then a staunch folk district.

"The cops couldn't believe for a minute that we didn't drink or do drugs," he also recalls, "but I wasn't dropping out of anything. I was a young businessman. I loved rock and roll, and there were a lot of other people who really wanted to be out and around after midnight. Obviously some bottles got smuggled in, but our bouncers pretty much kept good order. We never got busted. We were all too innocent and naive and into the music. People like Little Eva [famous for 'The Loco-Motion' of 1962] performed at the club. [Soul singer] Solomon Burke came over. We had Doris Troy ['Just One Look' of 1963] – you know, medium-rank but certainly well-known rock artists. I'd invite them back from a concert, and they would do a number or two, or they'd lip-synch something, and then my house band, or some of the other acts who were around at that time, would do the primary entertainment."

One night, Sonny Thomas and the Fabulous Shays showed up asking to replace the house band. Roman vividly recalls the moment.

"David came in and basically said he just wanted a chance to show what he could do. He said if I thought these guys were good I had a real surprise coming – that he could definitely cut these guys eight ways to Sunday. My band wasn't too happy, because this was a guy who was considered to be quite capable of taking care of himself in any set of circumstances. He had a big reputation. I mean, he did do time. For me this was really interesting company to be keeping, but after much cajoling and dickering, and after much protest, the house band let David up to play. And he was just fabulous. Blew everybody away."

Clayton-Thomas had a spine-chilling effect on audiences. He possessed a strangely intense vocal power – at once angry, sensuous, raw, and vulnerable. His later Blood, Sweat & Tears style sounds almost bland by comparison. Roman immediately wanted to record him. The only problem was that the Canadian recording industry was virtually non-existent at the time. "Everybody talked big," Roman says, "but show them a talent like David and they didn't know what to do." Roman responded by becoming a record producer himself. With two associates he formed Red Leaf Records, and in the summer of 1964 he recorded David Clayton-Thomas and the Shays, as they then called themselves, performing an R&B version of a John Lee Hooker song, "Boom Boom."

Almost instantly the song hit charts across the country, "Which gave us the idea," Roman says, "that this was easy as pie." Over the next 15 months he released three more singles: "Walk That Walk," "Take Me Back," and "Out of the Sunshine." All became Canadian hits, which in those days meant 10,000 or more copies sold. Receipts did not cover production costs, but on the strength of "Walk That Walk" the group travelled to New York to appear on a network-television program, *Hullabaloo.* For Clayton-Thomas the trip changed everything.

"We were in New York for three days," he says, "and I heard more music in those three days than I'd heard in my entire life. Greenwich Village, the East Side, the go-go bars uptown with Joey Dee and the Starliters, jazz like I'd never heard in my life. I was ruined. I knew I had to get back to New York."

Realizing that the Shays did not share his ambitions, Clayton-Thomas left them and formed, in Toronto, what he thought of as a "New York–type band," made up of jazz-trained musicians who could rock. He began with a brilliant young keyboard player named Tony Collacott.

"Tony was one of those Roman candles who burn out very early but was terribly gifted," Clayton-Thomas says. "He had played Carnegie Hall at age 15 with Sarah Vaughan, and I had seen him play with his own jazz trios. One day we bumped into each other in a sidewalk café and started talking, and I thought, 'What if a musician of his education, of his incredible virtuosity, was to play pop music, which is my field, and if he did, what kind of music would he play?' My conception of it was a very blues-based music with a level of musicality that just didn't exist in those days, rock being basically a three-chord, uneducated form that just kind of clanks along and the vocal is the whole thing. You know, 'I bought a guitar in a day or two, learned to play it in a week or two.' I think that's a Chuck Berry lyric.

"Rock music," he continues, "was just beginning to make the transition from the basic Chuck Berry, Memphis, New Orleans, three-chord, good-time rock and roll to something with a lot more literacy. I'm talking about George Martin and the Beatles, who took rock way beyond its 'Roll Over Beethoven' beginnings to albums like *Rubber Soul* [December 1965] and *Revolver* [August 1966], records that were exploring orchestrations and taking a much deeper musical approach, mostly because of the presence of George Martin, who was a BBC symphony conductor. The Beatles were a tremendous influence on all of us, and I wanted to incorporate this young jazz musician Collacott into an R&B band, and write our own music, and start in a very independent direction."

The café conversation took place in early 1966, and out of it came a new band, the Bossmen. By then Brave New World was history. It had lasted only a year and a half as Roman turned his spare-time interests away from running a club to producing records. He now had his own independent label, Roman Records, which proceeded to record the Bossmen performing a new Clayton-Thomas/ Collacott composition, "Brainwashed."

"Looking back on it," Clayton-Thomas says, "I realize that 'Brainwashed' was our first attempt at jazz-rock. We set up the basic jazz trio – piano, bass, and drums – and in direct contrast to having two guitars strum along to the keyboard lines, we orchestrated three guitars to play horn lines against the rhythm section. I played guitar, and there were two other guitar players, and we wrote individual parts for them, all very jazz-influenced lines, and very carefully orchestrated. We actually went into the studio with the parts written out. If you listen to the way 'Brainwashed' breaks down, there are three contrapuntal guitar lines working throughout the whole thing, with a piano break in it. That was my first stumbling attempt to make rock music with really literate, educated musicians."

In July 1966, "Brainwashed" began its rise on the trend-setting CHUM Chart, remaining for nearly three months and peaking at number 6. "I was working at CKEY," Roman says, "which gave CHUM every reason in the world to ignore us, but David's records were too cutting-edge." Roman tried to get something going south of the border as well. He arranged distribution through Capitol

Records, attracting initial attention from *Billboard* magazine. But the song didn't take. "It was very, very, very ahead of its time," Roman says.

"Basically," says Clayton-Thomas, "it was an anti–Vietnam War song, which at that time was not a popular issue in the United States."

Unable to sustain a career on Canadian success alone, Clayton-Thomas longed more than ever to leave for New York. One night at the Riverboat coffeehouse in Yorkville, he saw one of his childhood heroes, John Lee Hooker. The two knew each other from "Boom Boom," and as they were talking after the show, Hooker said he would be opening the following week at the Café A Go-Go in Greenwich Village. "If you're in New York next week, why don't you come and play with me?" he asked.

Clayton-Thomas sold his car, hitchhiked to New York, and arrived at the Café A Go-Go only to learn that Hooker had not been heard from. The club's owner was desperate. Hooker was scheduled to open in a few hours. Could Clayton-Thomas fill in? "I'll get back to you," Clayton-Thomas said and walked across the street to the Tin Angel restaurant to look for musicians. By chance he met three of the best in the country: harmonica player Charlie Musselwhite, guitarist Michael Bloomfield, and bass player Harvey Brooks, who with Bloomfield the year before had helped launch Bob Dylan's transition to rock music with members of the Band. After rehearsing for just an hour and a half, the four opened that night as Charlie Musselwhite's Chicago South Side Blues Band.

They stayed together for several months, after which Bloomfield and Brooks formed the jazz-rock group Electric Flag, and Clayton-Thomas fell in with other well-educated, classically schooled, jazz-trained musicians of the type he had been mixing with in Toronto. Among them was Al Kooper, another former Dylan session player. He had recently formed Blood, Sweat & Tears, an experimental rock group that incorporated strong jazz elements and other sophisticated forms into a lineup of drums, bass, keyboards, guitar, and a four-man horn section. It was Clayton-Thomas's dream group, and when Kooper left in 1969 Clayton-Thomas joined as lead singer.

The band then released its groundbreaking album *Blood, Sweat & Tears*. It topped the U.S. album chart for seven weeks, sold more than two million copies, and won the Grammy for album of the year. Three songs from the record also became million-selling singles: "Spinning Wheel" (written by Clayton-Thomas), "And When I Die," and "You've Made Me So Very Happy."

For the next three years, until Clayton-Thomas left temporarily in 1972, Blood, Sweat & Tears continued to record and tour widely and to exert a major influence on rock music. Other jazz-rock bands such as Chicago suddenly attracted a following, and jazz trumpeter Miles Davis crossed to jazz-rock, bringing his huge audience to the new style. Only after 1975, after thinning into middle-of-the-road pop, did jazz-rock lose its status in the rock world.

Clayton-Thomas now lives comfortably in a large ranchhouse in New York's Catskill Mountains with his wife, Suzanne. "I want to make music that's real and honest," he says, still talking like the young man who fired up audiences at Brave New World. Several comeback attempts over the years have failed to regain him his initial success, but he continues to perform live with a stripped-down version of a band he still calls Blood, Sweat & Tears.

4

504 Huron Street

When she was 20 years old, penniless, and pregnant with a daughter she would later give up for adoption, Joni Mitchell lived in a rooming-house at 504 Huron Street, a few blocks west of the Yorkville café district.

The house is an expansive three-storey semidetached structure of dark-red terracotta and brick in a neighborhood full of grand old homes topped with turrets and gables. Current roomers call it "a dump," but when Mitchell lived there in the mid-1960s, it was still well maintained and beautiful. People called it "the hippie rooming-house" and the woman who ran it, "the hippie landlady."

Her real name is Vera Frenkel. She is an accomplished artist and teacher now, much celebrated for her video work and realist gallery installations, but in those days she was a printmaker starting out. Originally she was from Czechoslovakia. With her parents, she had

(Photo: John Goddard)

Current roomers call it "a dump," but when Joni Mitchell lived at 504 Huron Street in the mid-1960s the building was still well-maintained and beautiful. People called it "the hippie rooming house" and the woman who ran it "the hippie landlady."

fled the Nazi invasion to northern England, then to Montreal, where she grew up and later married. In 1962 she and her husband, Oded, moved to Toronto and rented the Huron Street house, subletting rooms as a source of income.

"I did run around barefoot, and I did wear long skirts and dresses," Frenkel says now of the "hippie" label. "I would be in my studio on the second floor, and people would knock on the door and say, 'Can we have our sheets?' or 'Somebody is staying over on the weekend, is there an extra bed?' That's how it went. We didn't provide meals, but we did provide linen and cleaned the rooms and took care of everything else. I think people felt comfortable there, and word got around. There was a lot of coming and going."

On the first floor lived a Nigerian prince who studied at the University of Toronto, and on the third lived a quiet airport worker who sometimes urinated out the window. Duke Redbird, a poet and the editor of a native publication, *The Thunderbird,* rented a room on the second floor, while two young painters, unknown to anybody else at first, moved into the basement and established a studio there. Frequent visitors included Hungarian-born poet Robert Zend and Hungarian-born fiction writer Stephen Vizinczey. Zend met his wife, Janine, at the house, and Vizinczey had his most famous fictional character take a room there. "We parked on Huron Street, a narrow tree-lined street of shabby, turreted, dark-red brick Victorian mansions converted into rooming houses," recounts Andras Vajda, the sex-obsessed protagonist of Vizinczey's 1965 novel, *In Praise of Older Women,* "and walked from door to door inquiring about rents."

Frenkel remembers clearly the night she first met Joni Mitchell. It was in August 1964. Frenkel was teaching a summer course at the Ontario College of Art, and after the final class she invited everybody back to her place.

"All the students felt the need to linger and hang out, so we went to my studio," she recalls. "There were 15 or 18 of us, and one of my neighbors, Abbott Anderson, came over to borrow a book of Rilke's poetry that I had mentioned to him. Abbott is an actor from Jamaica. He has a wonderful, wonderful, deep voice – we used to hear him sometimes on radio ads and voice-overs on television – and for some reason we all began singing. We probably weren't all that sober by that time. I remember I went down to the kitchen to get something, and I heard this sort of sweet, reedy voice coming from the bathroom. I looked in and there was Joni, sitting on the edge of the bathtub strumming her guitar, very basic chords, long blond hair, slim, lovely. I still don't know how she happened to be there, but the place did have an aura – people were always coming around – and I said, 'Why don't you come upstairs and sing with us?'

"At first she said no, she was just tuning her guitar. She was very shy. But then she did come up, and she and Abbott sang together. I had a guitar, so Abbott played my guitar and Joni played hers. There were two guitars going, and I can remember them singing, 'We are climbing Jacob's ladder,' an old folk song, with her sweet soprano and his really resonant bass-baritone. It was extraordinary. They really hit it off. He was this very tall, good-looking black man, and she was this sort of medium-sized, slim, golden-haired girl. It was a lovely, golden moment. I don't remember that we were particularly innocent or sentimental. We weren't. We were all very skeptical, sophisticated artists, but it was a celebration, and that's how it began. Joni moved into the house."

Abbott Anderson, who teaches theatre in high schools now, adds that people were also charmed that he and his duet partner shared the same last name. Joni Mitchell was Joni Anderson then. She was born in Fort Macleod, Alberta, near Lethbridge, and grew up mostly in Saskatoon, Saskatchewan. After high school, she studied for a year in Calgary at the Alberta College of Art, and played regularly at a coffeehouse there, the Depression. Then she took a train to Ontario. She went east, she has always said, to hear Buffy Sainte-Marie perform at the Mariposa Folk Festival, held that year in Toronto near the Exhibition grounds.

Mitchell stayed to try to make it as a star herself, but success must have seemed a long way off then. Frenkel and others retain poignant memories of Mitchell as a young artist struggling to form a musical identity in the face of poverty, occasional homesickness, and an unplanned pregnancy.

Of her poverty, Frenkel says that Mitchell was unable to afford $120 to join the musicians' union, restricting her to the one nonunion coffeehouse in Yorkville, the Half Beat Club, at 47 Avenue Road, since rebuilt as retail and office space.

"She was very, very poor," recalls Duke Redbird, who lived across the hall from her. "We were all in that situation, really, but I remember there were times when we would have some fruit or apples or something and we would share them with her, and she was always very, very grateful."

Of Mitchell's introspective side, Frenkel says, "I remember a very detailed photograph album that she brought with her, with pictures of herself as a high-school student, as a graduate, and with boyfriends – all of it annotated with little drawings and little phrases. It was very touching. A lot had gone into arranging these photographs."

Of how tirelessly Mitchell worked at the vocal ability for which she would later become internationally celebrated, Frenkel recalls, "She was teaching herself to move between the lower and higher registers and she was having trouble. There was some skittering, some kind of strain, but she was really working on it. She was very, very focused, and she developed an ability to take her voice in those two directions. She said she wanted very much not to be the poor man's Joan Baez."

And of the main complication in Mitchell's life at the time, Frenkel says, "Joni was pregnant while she was living in our house. Three of our tenants were pregnant in the same season. It seems there was a less-than-cautious approach to things. Joni was pregnant – I don't remember who the father was – and she was selling coats at Simpsons. That was how she earned her living, and she sang in the evenings from time to time.

"When she was about eight months pregnant, she moved out. I think she must have found a haven somewhere, and I have a vivid memory of seeing her one day after that in the Bank of Montreal, which we all used, at St. George and Bloor. I remember she had a very nice coat on, a sort of turquoise blue. She looked wonderful. I asked her how she was, and she patted her stomach and said, 'Flat.' She had had the baby. The father was living with her, and another man at the same time, all in the same room. They were putting somebody up, and I think it was very hard on her. The whole pregnancy, I think, had been hard on her, esthetically and emotionally and financially."

Mitchell gave birth to a daughter in early spring 1965, and gave up the girl for adoption – events she kept secret from her parents and almost everybody else for decades. Until recently, all that was publicly known about her early career was that, in June 1965, she met the American folk singer Chuck Mitchell at the Penny Farthing coffeehouse on Yorkville Avenue, and married him within 36 hours. In early August, she appeared at the Mariposa Folk Festival, held that year 40 miles north of the city at Innis Lake, where she gave her first major performance and introduced one of her most popular early songs, "Both Sides Now." "A beautiful, blond Joan Baez," wrote one reviewer intending praise.

(Photo: William Smith, Mariposa Collection)

Joni Mitchell plays an afternoon concert at the 1966 Mariposa Folk Festival north of Toronto at Innis Lake, accompanied by Toronto guitarist David Rae. On the same stage one year earlier, she introduced "Both Sides Now," in the first major performance of her career.

Afterwards, she and Chuck moved to Detroit. They performed together as a duo on the Michigan folk-club circuit for a year and a half, until the marriage dissolved and she moved alone to New York. By then, she was becoming known as a songwriter. Tom Rush and Buffy Sainte-Marie had recorded her songs, and in 1968 Mitchell released her own self-titled album.

The same year she moved to California, and the next year she released her second album, *Clouds,* which included "Both Sides Now" and "Chelsea Morning." It won a Grammy award for best folk album. A year after that, in 1970, she released *Ladies of the Canyon,* featuring "Woodstock," "The Circle Game," and "Big Yellow Taxi" — songs that helped define the giddy momentum of the late 1960s and early 1970s and helped elevate her to star status, a voice of her generation.

Her next album was *Blue.* Released in 1971 and still cited frequently as her masterpiece, it drew attention for its musical sophistication and intense, diarylike intimacy. All the songs seem to probe Mitchell's feelings of loneliness, regret, anger, and abandonment.

One of them, "Little Green," tells of a mother who gives up her baby girl for adoption. Green would be a good name for the child, the song's narrator says, because the birth came in early spring, and because the parents were so green with inexperience as to be almost children themselves. "Weary of lies you are sending home," Mitchell sings in a heartbreaking, crystal-clear voice, "so you sign all the papers in the family name. You're sad and you're sorry, but you're not ashamed. Little Green, have a happy ending."

Mitchell continued to write and record, and to influence others. Phases of her work have been closely documented — her movement away from folk music into experimental styles of rock and jazz, and her switch from personal themes to social and political ones. On her 1982 album *Wild Things Run Fast,* however, another apparent reference to her daughter appears. "Now your kids are coming up straight," she sings as though to an old friend, "and my child's a stranger. I bore her, but I could not raise her."

In 1994, she released *Turbulent Indigo,* her seventeenth album, hailed as a return to her early form. It earned two Grammy awards, one for best pop album, the other for art direction (for her paintings on the cover and jacket sleeves). Other awards followed. In 1996, *Billboard* magazine conferred on her the Century Award for Distinguished Achievement, recognizing "uncommon excellence [in] an artist's unfolding body of work," and the King of Sweden presented her with the ultimate accolade – the Nobel Prize of music, the Polar Prize.

To help promote the new record, Mitchell gave a rare round of interviews, in which she publicly broached the subject of her daughter for the first time. A tabloid newspaper had published news about a "love child," and a couple of interviewers asked about the story. In one response, Mitchell seemed to suggest she did not give up the child right away.

"I had had a child," she told Charles Gandee of *Vogue* magazine. "I was broke, literally penniless, and I met Chuck Mitchell, and he said he would take us on. I was kind of railroaded … we were never suitable. I went down the aisle saying, 'I can get out of this.'"

In another response, she seemed to suggest that she had given the baby up earlier, but in both accounts she is clear about having had no other option, testimony to her desperate circumstances while living in Toronto. "I was dirt poor," she told Pamela Wallin on CBC's *Pamela Wallin Live.* "I mean I was on-the-street poor, I didn't have a penny … So I became the housekeeper for these two guys. You know, I had some friends, so it wasn't that rough, but it was difficult parting with the child. I had no money for diapers, or a room to take her to, so I had to let her go. I had no choice. There was no career on the horizon. I couldn't get work. Three years later I had a recording contract and a house and a car, but how could I see that in the future?"

"Have you ever looked for her?" Wallin asked.

"I started to on a couple of occasions but I ran into real ugly attitudes" – because of her fame and money – "and backed off … The last time I was in Toronto, after the cat was out of the bag, the foster mother who had her for the first few months, who was an old woman by that time, recognized my bone structure on television and mailed me all her early baby pictures. So I have that. I think about her from time to time. I hope she's all right."

5

The Sparrow's Nest

153 ST. GEORGE STREET, APARTMENT 706

On the top floor of a modest, high-rise apartment building two blocks west of Yorkville, John Kay and Mars Bonfire began a musical collaboration that led, years later, to one of the biggest rock anthems of all time – "Born to Be Wild." Bonfire wrote the song, Kay sang it with Steppenwolf, and the rebel-biker image implicit in the lyrics became a permanent part of Kay's rock persona.

Kay first cultivated a rebel image while attending high school at Humberside Collegiate in the city's west end. The year was 1958. Kay was Joachim Krauledat then, a Grade 9 student freshly emigrated from West Germany with his mother and stepfather to an apartment at 140 Quebec Avenue, near High Park. He remembers feeling lonely there. He was a bright, sensitive boy, who spoke almost no English and was legally blind. He was also acutely nearsighted, and his eyes were so light-sensitive that he had to wear sunglasses all the time. He became the only student at Humberside allowed to wear dark glasses to class, a distinction that bestowed on him a cool, rebellious look, which he emphasized by adding motorcycle boots and a black leather jacket.

"I definitely stuck out," he says in his 1994 autobiography, *John Kay: Magic Carpet Ride,* but he also remained isolated. For solace he turned to music. He listened to records and to U.S. radio stations, from which he also heard the news of Buddy Holly's death in a plane crash in February 1959. "I was stunned," he says. "For teenagers then, music was almost everything." Certainly it was almost everything to him. He talked his mother into buying him a Kay guitar from Simpsons department store, and practised constantly. He went to all-ages Saturday matinées at rock clubs to watch such groups as Ronnie Hawkins and the Hawks, the city's top band, and took a part-time job at Maple Leaf Gardens selling peanuts at concerts staged by Dick Clark's touring Caravan of Stars. By the time he graduated from Humberside in 1963, Kay knew he wanted to be a rock star himself.

That summer his family moved to Buffalo. He started going to folk clubs there, and developed musically to the point where he was invited to play in some. His world began to expand. With a friend, he drove to California, where he mixed with such emerging musicians as Taj Mahal, Tim Hardin, Roger McGuinn, and David Crosby. In 1965, after two years away, he returned to Toronto. The Yorkville coffeehouse scene was in full swing, and Kay landed a regular spot at the Half Beat Club, just up from the Purple Onion. He billed himself as "John Kay from California." One night, a member of a band called the Sparrows asked if he wanted to sit in with them, and Kay's world expanded further.

"I liked the fuller sound that a band offered," he says. "There was an intensity and excitement that was absent from performing solo on acoustic guitar … Being part of a band increased the possibility of success, perhaps making records."

The Sparrows had named themselves in comic homage to the Hawks. A few months earlier, as Jack London and the Sparrows, they had scored a local hit with "If You Don't Want My Love," but London had since left and the remaining band members were trying to replace him. The core members were two brothers from nearby Oshawa, Dennis and Jerry McCrohan. They called themselves Dennis and Jerry Edmonton, and later Dennis changed his name again to Mars Bonfire. He played lead guitar, wrote songs, and sang ballads. Jerry played drums and sang Rolling Stones and Manfred Mann hits. A keyboard player, Goldy McJohn, and a bassist, Nick St. Nicholas, also helped with vocals, but the group was looking for a lead singer who could bring them a heavier, bluesier sound.

"Nick and my brother Jerry were very aware that we needed a stronger singer than any of us were," Bonfire recalls from his home in California. "We were kind of light vocalists, roughly in the style of the Beatles. They would scout around the clubs every weekend to see what was available, and they became aware of John Kay, who was performing as a solo blues singer in the style of John Hammond Jr. They were very impressed with his voice, and he also played the harmonica and had a unique style on the guitar."

In mid-September 1965, the Sparrows invited Kay to join the group, and he accepted. They also asked him to move in with them. Dennis, Jerry, and Nick were sharing an apartment at 153 St. George Street, suite 706, on the top floor of a buff-colored building at the corner of Lowther Avenue. (McJohn, the keyboard player, lived with his father.) Having Kay around all the time meant that he and Dennis (Mars Bonfire) could rehearse guitar parts they had to learn together.

"When he joined," Bonfire says, "we carried on doing some of the songs that we did best as the Sparrows, with the same vocalists who were doing them before. Those songs were roughly in the English style, and I showed them to John. Then he taught us a bunch of songs that he knew. We kind of split it 50–50. He learned the more pop of our stuff, and we learned a lot of his stuff, and went more in a blues direction."

"Because we all lived together," says Kay in his book, "we could spend more time working songs out. These guys were well organized. Everybody seemed to have a role. Jerry was the treasurer, looking after all the bills. Dennis was practising a lot, developing his guitar chops and songwriting. Nick was the hustler, dealing with the agents and getting the gigs. I did a lot of playing with Dennis and started to write more."

A routine developed. On most days the band members walked the couple of blocks east to Yorkville for a late breakfast, rehearsed in the afternoon at whatever club they might be playing, stopped for dinner, returned to the club at around 9, finished at midnight or so, and hung around until all hours with other musicians and hangers-on. Usually they played Yorkville during the week and out-of-town dances on weekends.

By the spring of 1966 they wanted more. In April they drove to New York to make a demo tape, and shortened their name to the Sparrow – "to give it a more hip ring," Kay says. In June they returned to New York for an extended club engagement. In the fall they were still there, but by then the action had shifted to California. They faced a choice: retreat to Toronto or keep moving. With winter on the way, they headed west in a loaded station wagon.

For the next six months, the Sparrow struggled to find a place for themselves in the emerging California hippie culture, first in Los Angeles, then in San Francisco. They dropped acid, and dropped the more pop-oriented material from their repertoire in favor of drawn-out, experimental versions of such songs as "The Pusher," a Hoyt

Axton number that Kay had adopted almost as his own. The San Francisco scene was hopping. The top acts were the Grateful Dead, Moby Grape, Jefferson Airplane, and Big Brother and the Holding Company, with Janis Joplin. The Sparrow ranked way down the list. "For the whole duration of our stay in San Francisco, we never rose much beyond second billing at the Avalon and the Fillmore," says Kay. "We never got beyond being considered the new kids who blew in from out of town."

In the spring of 1967, the eve of the Summer of Love, the Sparrow disbanded. Nick went his own way. Kay, Jerry Edmonton, and McJohn returned to Los Angeles hoping to form a new band. Dennis Edmonton moved to Los Angeles to join Leeds Music as a staff songwriter.

For Dennis, it was a happy time. He rented a small apartment in Hollywood and enjoyed himself by riding around in his first car, a second-hand Ford Falcon. It was during this period that he changed his name. He took Mars from a book he was reading on Greek mythology, Mars being the Greek god of war. He got Bondfire, then Bonfire, after watching several James Bond movies in a row.

In the same haphazard way, he was inventing and creating songs. "I was walking down Hollywood Boulevard one day," he recalls of his most famous composition, "and saw a poster in a window saying 'Born to Ride' with a picture of a motorcycle erupting out of the earth like a volcano with all this fire around it. All this came together lyrically in my head – the idea of the motorcycle coming out, along with the freedom and joy I felt in having my first car and being able to drive myself around whenever I wanted."

From the sensation of driving a used Ford came the quintessential biker song, "Born to Be Wild." Quietly, so as not to disturb his neighbors, Bonfire sang it into a borrowed tape recorder while playing an unplugged Telecaster. Shortly afterwards, Jerry called. A new

John Kay of Steppenwolf speaks at a Toronto news conference in March 1996 prior to his induction into the Canadian Music Hall of Fame. Wearing a black leather jacket, dark glasses and wolf insignia on his lapel, he continues to project the rebel image he cultivated as a student at Humberside Collegiate.

band was coming together. Did Bonfire have any songs? Bonfire dropped off the tape, and in one afternoon the band worked out the now-famous high-powered arrangement, complete with opening drum crack and driving guitar riff.

"Did I realize at the time that it might have any significance, or was special in any way?" Bonfire asks rhetorically. "The honest answer is that at the time I was very actively involved in writing – writing maybe a song or two a day – and I liked them all. From my point of view, it was just another song."

For the band members, "Born to Be Wild" meant much more. In the same savage, untamable spirit of the song's theme, they took the name Steppenwolf, German for "wolf of the Steppes," and landed a record deal. Months passed, but in June 1968 the record company released "Born to Be Wild" as a single, and Steppenwolf scored its monster first hit.

"It was summertime," Kay says to partly explain the success. "Kids were out of school and wanted to hear more exciting, get-it-on, high-energy music. The song became an anthem for any kid tooling around on the highway or hitting the road. It also came out at a very turbulent period, the summer of 1968 – the Vietnam War on television every night, student demonstrations on campuses, the Martin Luther King and Bobby Kennedy assassinations, urban rioting, the Chicago convention. The song's lyrics and message spoke to a generation which craved some excitement and some escape."

The following year, in 1969, "Born to Be Wild" and "The Pusher" were picked for the soundtrack of *Easy Rider,* the hit road movie about two drug freaks "in search of America" on Harley-Davidsons. The film's success further enhanced Kay's leather-and-sunglasses mystique, and spread the Steppenwolf name worldwide.

6 Wash and Dry Self-Serve Laundry

167 DUPONT STREET

"Zol and Denny working for a penny," sing the Mamas and the Papas in their autobiographical 1967 hit, "Creeque Alley."

Zol is Zal (pronounced Zol) Yanovsky, the lead guitarist and co-founder, with John Sebastian, of the Lovin' Spoonful, who rode the top of the charts from mid-1965 to late 1967 with such hits as "Do You Believe in Magic," "You Didn't Have to Be So Nice," and "Summer in the City." Denny is Denny Doherty, perhaps best known as the clear tenor that carries "Monday, Monday," a number 1 hit by the Mamas and the Papas in early 1966, following closely on the heels of their smash debut single, "California Dreamin'." Zal and Denny worked for pennies in Toronto, moved south together, and branched off to help form two of the hottest folk-rock acts of the 1960s.

Yanovsky is a Toronto boy. By the time he was 16, in 1961, he was living on his own at 125 Dupont Street, just west of Avenue Road, in a house now partly occupied by the offices of the literary agent Denise Bukowski. His main hangout was the Wash and Dry laundromat a couple of blocks farther west at 167 Dupont, now Phoenix Video. It was warm, it was cheap, it was open 24 hours a day, and it was handy to another hangout, the Dupont Coffee Shop, now a Coffee Time Donuts, at the corner of Dupont and St. George Streets.

Yanovsky once told a writer that he actually lived in the laundromat until Doherty hired him. "I was catapulted from the dryer to the stage of the Colonial Tavern," he told Martin Melhuish for the 1983 book *Heart of Gold: 30 Years of Canadian Pop Music.* Now he says the story is not literally true, but as owner of a deli and the Chez Piggy restaurant in Kingston, Ontario – his rock-music days far behind him – he says he prefers not to reminisce.

Doherty is not as reticent. He is now a television actor living in suburban Toronto, and recalls his own itinerant Toronto days with the effusiveness for which both he and Yanovsky were once so famous. "What?" he says. "Get a lease? Get a landlord? No, man, we were gypsies. We were vagabonds. We slept wherever we could sleep. Be ready to move. Have your gear packed and your guitar case ready to go. We were just passing through, man."

During one period, he says, he stayed in a house at the southeast corner of Bloor and Huron Streets, where the experimental Rochdale College went up a few years later, at the height of hippiedom. "A big old Victorian brick house," Doherty recalls. "There was an apartment on the top floor, and a couple of English girls would allow me and a guitar player, Eric Horde, to sleep on their floor. Later, I kept thinking about Rochdale, how crazy it was, and how appropriate that they put it up where we used to live."

Doherty is from Halifax. From 1955 to 1958, he sang in a rock-and-roll band called the Hepsters, then switched to folk music "because it was a way to make a living and get out of town," he says. He helped form a group called the Colonials, with a guitar player, a washtub-bass player, and himself on lead vocals. "We were sort of like the Kingston Trio – a commercial folk act trying to get by," he says with his typical mix of modesty and enthusiasm. "We had a lot of stuff that we had written ourselves, and that the purists looked down their noses on us for but, hey, we'd go right on through."

In 1960, the Colonials left Halifax for Montreal. A year later, they went to Toronto to appear on *Juliette,* the CBC music show aired Saturday nights after *Hockey Night in Canada.* After that, other work kept coming their way.

"We played the Colonial Tavern, and we were the first to play the Las Vegas Room at the Seaway Hotel [since demolished]," Doherty says. "We also worked the Imperial Room at the Royal York Hotel, and there were about three coffeehouses at that time – the House of Hamburg, the Village Corner Club, and the Bohemian Embassy.

"The hootenannies at the Bohemian Embassy were things of wonder," he continues. "Ian and Sylvia would get up and do a couple of numbers. We would get up and do a couple. We'd do all these folk sets going, 'Tra-la-la, la-la-la-la-la.' But after you got up at the hoot at the Bohemian Embassy, you'd go, 'Is there any place else to work?' The folk clubs were selling coffee and cake. They weren't making enough money to pay everybody, so you would pass the hat, or play for nothing, and hope that somebody had heard you or hope something magical would happen, because that's what you wanted to do. And there was nothing else, so you would go down to New York and play on Bleecker Street in the Village for baskets. You would pass the basket after doing a set, and you could pick up 25 or 30 bucks, and if you did that two or three times a night, you could live.

"You couldn't do that up here," Doherty continues. "There was a folk scene here, but nobody knew that yet. Gordon Lightfoot was here. David Wiffen. Carol Robinson and Amos Garrett were hanging out – this was before the Dirty Shames. Zal was here playing his Goya gut-string guitar.

"When I met Zal, he had just gotten back from a kibbutz in Israel, where he had blown the tracks off a Caterpillar tractor by putting the brakes on it at 20 or 30 miles an hour. You're supposed to gear them down, but he put the brakes on, blew the brakes, and destroyed several buildings on the kibbutz. He went right through the mess hall or something, which they had just finished building, and they said, 'Don't help us any more. Israel can get by without you. This is one Jew who should go home.'

"So he came back to Toronto. He was hanging out, we were hanging out, and we needed a guitar player. Our guitarist only played chords, so we needed somebody who could pick some melodies, and Zal could do that, so we picked him up. Then the washtub player left, and we were down to three again."

Sometime in 1963, the Colonials relocated to Greenwich Village. Two lines from the song "Creeque Alley" tell of the decision: "Zolly said, 'Denny, you know there aren't many who can sing a song the way that you do – let's go south.' Denny said, 'Zolly, golly, don't you think that I wish I could play guitar like you?'"

An agent suggested a name change. The Colonials sounded too much like a throwback to the Thirteen Colonies, he said, suggesting instead the Halifax Three to conform in style to the Kingston Trio and the Brothers Four. "We said, 'You give us the dates and you can call us anything you want,'" Doherty recalls.

In New York, he and Yanovsky met all the members of their two future respective groups. They met Cass Elliot of the Big Three, and John and Michelle Phillips of the Journeymen, all three of whom would later form the Mamas and the Papas with Doherty. In February 1964, Cass Elliot invited friends over to watch the Beatles' first appearance on *The Ed Sullivan Show*. Among them were Yanovsky and Sebastian, who ended up playing guitars together until dawn.

The new formations took place in stages. Yanovsky, Doherty, and Elliot played in a group together. Sebastian joined them briefly. Doherty formed a group with John and Michelle Phillips. Finally,

Former Lovin' Spoonful vocalist John Sebastian (centre) congratulates Zal Yanovsky (left) and Denny Doherty on their induction in 1996 into the Canadian Music Hall of Fame. Yanovsky and Doherty played together in Toronto and New York before splitting to help form two of the hottest folk-rock acts of the 1960s — the Lovin' Spoonful and the Mamas and the Papas.

(Photo: Catherine Sebastian)

Yanovsky and Sebastian teamed up with two other players to form the Lovin' Spoonful in New York. Elliot moved to California, and Doherty, John, and Michelle joined her there.

At the 1996 Canadian music awards, the Junos, Yanovsky and Doherty were inducted into the Canadian Music Hall of Fame. On hand to present the awards to them, respectively, were John Sebastian and Michelle Phillips.

7

The Concert Hall

888 YONGE STREET

The Concert Hall occupies part of a spooky building at Yonge Street and Davenport Road formerly known as the Masonic Temple. From 1918 until recently, the upper floor remained the exclusive realm of the secret society of Free and Accepted Masons, a place of windowless meeting chambers with ceilings 20 feet high, occult symbols carved into doorknobs, and bodies buried in the floors.

In 1993, the Masons sold the building to another secret society called the Rosedale Group, an entertainment company whose owners are known only to themselves. Their plan is to convert the temple into an all-purpose facility for trade exhibits, fund-raising events, and weddings. The owners are proceeding in stages. The first came in 1995, when they reopened the Concert Hall, a cavernous room on the main floor, long accessible to the public for musical events. It has a celebrated history. Bing Crosby and Frank Sinatra have each performed there, as have David Bowie and Boy George. But mostly the Concert Hall is renowned for its brief period of glory in the late 1960s as the Rock Pile.

San Francisco had the Fillmore. New York City had the Fillmore East. Toronto had the Rock Pile. It opened on September 23, 1968, with Blood, Sweat & Tears, the first band in a stellar parade of rock and blues acts that soon included Chuck Berry, Howlin' Wolf, John Mayall, and the Paul Butterfield Blues Band. Muddy Waters and John Lee Hooker once shared a double bill there, and the Who once tried out early material for their eventual rock opera, *Tommy*.

Led Zeppelin played the Rock Pile twice, and it is their name in particular that is so indelibly associated with the club's short existence. They first appeared there on February 2, 1969, just three weeks after the North American release of their first album, *Led Zeppelin*. They were not well known. Advertisements billed the band as "Led Zeppelin featuring Jimmy Page," recognizable as the guitar hero from the Yardbirds.

Led Zeppelin's second Rock Pile appearance came six months later, on August 18. Between the time they accepted the booking and the actual concert date, they had taken North America by storm. "Good Times Bad Times" had scored a hit, and the group was blowing audiences

(Poster courtesy of George Ungar)

A poster announces the notorious Led Zeppelin concert of August 18, 1969, opened by local blues band Edward Bear. Clockwise from the top are: Jimmy Page (lead guitar), Robert Plant (vocals), John Paul Jones (bass) and John Bonham (drums).

away with transcendent interpretations of Willie Dixon numbers such as "I Can't Quit You Baby" and "You Shook Me," on which lead singer Robert Plant would duel vocally with Page's Sunburst Les Paul. Two shows at the Rock Pile were scheduled. Both were oversold. Richard Flohil, a longtime blues fan and promoter, went as a guest of John Brower, one of the club's owners. Flohil tells what happened next.

"Peter Grant, who was their manager and has since passed on to his reward, which I think will be about 50 long millenniums in hell, walked into the office where I and a bunch of other people were hanging around and said, basically, 'Look, guys, this isn't good enough. We're going to need more money.'

"Peter Grant was physically big," Flohil continues. "He was a brawler, he was an excellent wrestler, and he had the morals of a scum bag. I mean, the guy was a menace. He mellowed in his old age and became sort of reflective about all that, but really the guy was impossible. He had been outside and had seen the lineup, which was literally around the block. There were 1,500 people all trying to get into a place that comfortably holds 700 or 800, and there were already 1,500 people jammed in there. Peter said, 'I want more money,' and John Brower or somebody said, 'Well, sorry, but we've got a contract and here it is.'

"Peter said, 'Can I have a look at that?' So they passed it over to him, and he just ripped it to shreds. I'll never forget it. He was standing over everybody wearing a white shirt with his British passport sticking out of the shirt pocket, and he just said, 'Screw you. We're not going on until you deliver the money. See ya. You deal with the riot.'

"So the owners paid up, and although I did not see this – I heard about it later – a sort of war started up between the club's people and the band's people. Somebody from the club stole the distributor cap from the band's truck and said, in effect, 'Okay, guys, give us our money back and you can have your equipment.'

"But I think sheer weight of numbers defeated that one. The club knew that if they didn't pay, and the band didn't go on, there would be a riot inside and a riot outside. I mean, it was craziness."

The show did go on, but Peter Grant's extortion crippled the owners, and the Rock Pile immediately closed.

8

The Purple Onion

35 AVENUE ROAD

The Purple Onion thrived in the mid-1960s as a Yorkville folk club. It was painted purple on the outside, and occupied a prime location – the north half of a Victorian double house at the northeast corner of Yorkville Avenue and Avenue Road. Both halves now constitute Alan Cherry, a swish women's clothing shop. The scuffed floor on which folkies once butted unfiltered cigarettes now gleams with polished marble. The dim hall once crammed with tables and chairs now displays dresses hanging brightly under track lighting. Even the basement has been refurbished. Instead of bare steps leading to a grotto, a carpeted staircase now sweeps to a lower level filled with gowns priced at hundreds of dollars each. The room has completely changed, but it was here in late 1963 that Buffy Sainte-Marie wrote "The Universal Soldier," a song about personal choice that became one of the most subversive protest anthems of the Vietnam War.

"I was travelling around," she now recalls of the days leading to her arrival at the club. "I don't remember where I had been, but I had to go through San Francisco – one of those flights where you had to spend the night at the airport and the next flight doesn't leave until 6 a.m. So I was at San Francisco airport in the middle of the night, and I saw soldiers carrying their buddies in on stretchers, all bandaged up. I started talking to some of these soldiers, and as we were talking I started thinking, 'Who is responsible for war, anyway? Is it these guys?'"

In those days, Vietnam was little talked about. American servicemen stationed in the south were said to be advisers only, and although their ranks were already escalating, the numbers were small compared to the hundreds of thousands of American troops involved after 1965.

"The war was very much underground, but those soldiers knew there was a war," Sainte-Marie says. "A lot of other people had an awareness of it, too, and there was a sense of wanting to do something – not stick our tongues out at the soldiers so much as bring our brothers home. There was a sense that war was wrong, and 'Why don't we stop using our friends as cannon fodder against somebody else's friends for reasons we don't even believe in?'"

On the flight to Toronto, Sainte-Marie continued to turn the questions over in her mind: Who is responsible for war? Were those soldiers responsible? "To a certain extent I thought they were," she says. "They were the people who point the guns, the professional soldiers who make a career of being in the military. But thinking about it further, I thought, 'Who is it that points the army? The generals. But who has the responsibility of declaring war? The politicians.' Then I thought, 'Wait a minute. Who elects the politicians? Oh, oh – it's us.'"

Late that afternoon, Sainte-Marie arrived alone at the Purple Onion wearing a trench coat and a pair of sneakers, shivering with cold. She carried her guitar in a cardboard case. "I went in and set up the sound," she recalls, "then went down into the basement to wait until it was time to play. That's when I wrote the song."

The soldier of the title is of any age and height, of any nationality and religion, fighting for any cause. "He's the Universal Soldier," the lyrics go, "and he really is to blame. His orders come from far away no more. They come from him, and you and me, and brothers can't you see, this is not the way to put an end to war."

No mention is made of Vietnam. "I wanted the song to make sense to any person in the world, in any language it was sung in, for a long time," Sainte-Marie says.

"The song," she also says, "is really about taking individual responsibility for most everything. In a working democracy, we are all ultimately responsible for what happens. You can't just blame the generals. In a democracy, if we are not vigilant enough ourselves to make our dreams come true, we can't expect politicians to do any better."

Here she is speaking not only about the song, but also about the philosophy she lives by. Sainte-Marie believes in individual choice and empowerment. From early adulthood, she assumed responsibility for her own happiness to the point where questions of blame and the inadequacies of others became irrelevant. She never knew who her natural parents were, she says, only that she was born in 1941 on the Piapot Reserve near Regina, Saskatchewan, and adopted as an infant by an American couple who were part Micmac. They lived in Wakefield, Massachusetts, north of Boston, and spent summers in a trailer at Sebago Lake, Maine. Her adoptive father was a refrigerator mechanic, her adoptive mother an occasional waitress. Sainte-Marie grew up frightened and alone.

"It wasn't possible to be an Indian where I lived," she once said. "People thought Indians were dead, or stuffed like wolves or eagles." Teachers told her that she was French, because of her family name, and hit her when she questioned whether Columbus truly discovered America. Her parents also dismissed her native identity. Worse, they abused her. "I was timid and scared and terrified because I was getting knocked around a lot," she told *Today* magazine in 1981. "I kept my mouth shut – at home, in school and in the neighborhood. I was a real loner … I was hurt and disgusted by the world. I felt like a blank cheque. So I'd pray: 'If You have anything for me to do, then I'm volunteering.'"

Gradually, Sainte-Marie discovered that her purpose lay in music. "Music was a place I went when I felt too much anger, love, or confusion," she once said. When she was three, a discarded piano became her closest companion. Sometimes, when left alone in the house, she listened to an old record player, and her only record, *Swan Lake,* channelling the faint sound to her ears through vacuum-cleaner tubes, like giant earphones. Constantly she heard original songs in her head – "like a radio playing," she says – and when she was 12, she bought a guitar from a second-hand store, teaching herself to play "all backwards," with her own finger patterns, and tuning differently for every song.

"To me, creativity is the true gospel," she often tells concert audiences now. "All of us are creative. The solutions to most of the problems in the world are already inside us."

At 17, Sainte-Marie left Wakefield in search of a better life. She travelled first to the Piapot Cree Reserve to find her parents, and when nobody could establish who they might be, she chose Emile Piapot and Claire Starblanket as her new adoptive ones. They accepted her in a formal community ceremony, an act that began her lifelong connection to the Piapot Cree and to the rest of Canada. "If I couldn't change the old world, I could help create a new one," she once said. "My adoption into the tribe gave me a new childhood, a new life."

Afterwards, she entered the University of Massachusetts and began circulating with other active, creative people. In 1963, she graduated with an elementary-school teacher's certificate and an honors degree in Oriental philosophy. She also won a scholarship to study in India. She planned to go, she says, but decided first to spend the summer in New York, "just for the heck of it – to see what it would be like to play my songs there." She played at the Gaslight Café, and Gerde's Folk City, and in the fall put off going to India to travel instead to folk clubs and university campuses throughout North America.

"I was part of the whole singer-songwriter movement of the early sixties," she says now. "I was just a college girl with a guitar, travelling around like a lot of other people. It was a different time. A lot of people were writing. It was no big deal to play the guitar and write songs. That's what music was to me, a source of empowerment for everybody."

The following year, in 1964, Sainte-Marie signed with Vanguard Records, the prestigious folk label that was recording Joan Baez and Ian and Sylvia. She released her first album, *It's My Way*, featuring "The Universal Soldier," an album that caused *New York Times* critic Robert Shelton to hail her as "one of the most promising new talents on the folk scene." She also drew acclaim at the Newport Folk Festival that year, and became the surprise hit of the Mariposa Folk Festival, held in Toronto that summer and starring blues pickers Reverend Gary Davis and Mississippi John Hurt. The crowd called her back four times.

Audiences warmed to Sainte-Marie partly for her stunning beauty. In 1964, *Look* magazine referred to her as "this sexy-ethereal creature," and *Time* made much of "her dusky face, framed by a cascade of raven hair that spills across her shoulders and down to her waist." (As recently as 1994, Lenny Stoute of the *Toronto Star* extolled her as "truly babe-acious.")

(Photo: Toronto Star)

Buffy Sainte-Marie rehearses in a Toronto hotel room prior to her sensational performance at the 1964 Mariposa Folk Festival, where the audience called her back four times. "I was just a college girl with a guitar, travelling around like a lot of other people," she says of the time.

Her voice won over audiences as well. It was strong and full-bodied. "A primitive vibrato," one critic called it, or as the *Time* reporter wrote: "She can purr, she can belt, she can shade her voice with an eerie tremble that crawls up the listener's spine."

Most alluring of all, perhaps, were the songs themselves. The British folk singer Donovan scored a hit with "The Universal Soldier" in 1965, turning it into one of the most famous songs of Sainte-Marie's early career and into what *Life* magazine called "the battle hymn of the draft card burners." Yet Sainte-Marie avoided being labelled strictly a protest singer. "I don't want to spend my life making people cry guilty tears in concert halls," she once said. Her broad repertoire included simple ditties such as "Cripple Creek," to which she accompanied herself on the Indian mouth-bow, and stirring love songs such as "Until It's Time for You to Go," later also recorded by Elvis Presley, Barbra Streisand, Sonny and Cher, and more than 200 other artists in 16 countries.

"Some of my songs are just love songs," she says. "They are what I still think of as college-girl songs, even some of the ones I write now – songs that are pretty to hear, or involve some nice guitar changes that make you want to dance. But I feel that my real art as a song-writer is the song that teaches something to the intellect and also moves the emotions, so that the person who hears the song actually feels moved to think or do something."

Over the next several years, Sainte-Marie continued to write and record a mix of simple songs and deeper ones, including such uncompromising native-rights numbers as "Now That the Buffalo's Gone," "Native North American Child," and "My Country 'Tis of Thy People You're Dying."

By the end of the 1960s she had released four more albums, including *Little Wheel Spin and Spin* (1966) and *I'm Gonna Be a Country Girl Again* (1968). In 1971, she scored a hit with the theme song to the film *Soldier Blue,* and over the next five years released five more albums. By then, however, disillusionment over changes in the late 1960s had begun to show in her work.

"The early sixties were about students, coffee, caffeine," Sainte-Marie says of the changing times. "The late sixties were more about alcohol, alcohol clubs, and the Mamas and the Papas. Business sort of got hold of something that started out to be very free, outspoken, and well thought out. The Mamas and the Papas were not really saying anything, but they had the look. Other groups, too – they sort of seemed like they might be saying something, but they didn't really come out of the student movement, they capitalized on it. The student movement was very rich – it was thoughtful, it was genuine, it was enthusiastic. People like Phil Ochs were writing very powerful songs, people who never really made it through the obsta-cle course into show business. All of that was capitalized on by the whole kind of Woodstock field, which was more about mass money than about having something to say."

In 1976, Sainte-Marie ceased recording indefinitely. By then, she was living in Hawaii with her second husband, Sheldon Wolfchild.

She took an on-camera job with *Sesame Street,* pleased with a chance to make Indian people visible to a mass children's audience, the way she wished they had been visible when she was a child. "We reach 52 countries every day," she said at the time, "and my presence says yes, we Indians exist, we're not a thing of the past."

She remained on the show for five years, during which she gave birth to a boy, Dakota Starblanket Wolfchild. Then her life changed again. Her marriage dissolved, and she married Jack Nitzsche, a record producer, and in 1982 both collaborated with Will Jennings to write "Up Where We Belong," the theme song to the movie *An Officer and a Gentleman.* The three composers won Academy Awards for best song.

Sainte-Marie says she never entirely stopped performing on Canadian reserves and U.S. reservations, but while her son was growing up, she spent most of her time at home looking after him and exploring computer uses for her music and visual art. In 1987, she also began to follow the Iran–Contra hearings on CNN. She watched as a retired U.S. general, Richard Secord, told a congressional committee that he had been involved in an illegal CIA operation to sell weapons to Iran. Part of the profits from the sales, Secord confessed, were being diverted to Nicaraguan Contra guerrillas working to overthrow their leftist government.

"I watched the hearings every day, and he impressed me," Sainte-Marie said of Secord not long afterwards. "I don't know why. He's the antithesis of me in terms of life experience, but I respected him. Just watching him you could see this brilliant, creative man, with this incredible loyalty." Coming at the subject another way, she also said, "I've always very naively looked down my nose at hawks, and I realize that that has been a failing in me spiritually. I have more compassion now for somebody who sees the world differently."

Secord's stark testimony stirred Sainte-Marie in the way that wounded soldiers being carried into San Francisco airport had stirred her a generation earlier. She went on a songwriting binge, penning dozens of compositions about corruption in high places among people she portrayed as essentially well-meaning. She wrote "Fallen Angels," "Disinformation," "Bad End," and "The Big Ones Get Away." At one point she even phoned Secord to tell him of the unexpected compassion his testimony aroused in her. "We've been great friends ever since," she says.

In 1992 she released a new album, *Coincidence and Likely Stories,* reviving her recording career after 16 years and regaining her public profile. The album features a mix of love tunes, powerful native-rights numbers backed by pow-wow drummers, and the best of the Secord-inspired songs.

"I feel that in order to put an end to war in the world, you have to put an end to the war in the human heart," Sainte-Marie said on the album's release, echoing the philosophy she first put forward in "The Universal Soldier." "That takes understanding, and most of us don't have much these days. We're just name-calling and 'them and us-ing.' But we don't have to do that. We can do better."

9

Nimbus 9 Productions

131 HAZELTON AVENUE

What is now a medical clinic treating ear problems once served as a recording studio to Alice Cooper, Ringo Starr, Pink Floyd, and a Winnipeg band that became the biggest noise in rock in 1970 – the Guess Who. The studio was Nimbus 9. It opened in 1968 as a simple production office near the corner of Hazelton Avenue and Davenport Road in Yorkville, with the Guess Who as its only client. Two years later, the group scored a giant hit with "American Woman," the first Canadian-produced record to reach number 1 on the U.S. *Billboard* chart. The group also notched two other hit singles that year – "Hand Me Down World" and "No Time" – and rode the album charts for the entire period with *American Woman*, the LP.

Sheer numbers tell the story. In 1970, the Guess Who sold more 45-rpm singles than any other group or solo artist in the world. In

1969–70, they scored five Top 10, million-selling U.S. singles in a row, registered a U.S. gold album, and held the number 1 spot with "American Woman" for three consecutive weeks, edging out "Let It Be" by the Beatles. Sales of their singles and albums for the two-year period reached 25 million units, more than all other Canadian artists combined, including Gordon Lightfoot and Anne Murray.

The breakthrough opened the way for others. Until 1970, a steady stream of musicians had moved south: Neil Young, Joni Mitchell, Ian and Sylvia, John Kay and Steppenwolf, David Clayton-Thomas, Levon and the Hawks. The Guess Who helped stem the tide. They showed that a band could attain international success while continuing to reside principally in Canada, and helped lay the groundwork, through Nimbus 9, for a high-quality domestic recording industry.

Yet the Guess Who make an odd success story. Formed in the early 1960s as Chad Allan and the Reflections, later changed to Chad Allan and the Expressions, they weaved a quirky path to the big time through talent, ingenuity, and prodigious runs of both good and bad luck. Early on they copied the British bands, particularly Cliff Richard and the Shadows, and got their first break in 1965 by recording an earlier British hit by Johnny Kidd and the Pirates, "Shakin' all Over."

Unable to afford proper recording facilities, the group rented a Winnipeg television studio. They arrived late at night after rehearsing all day and performing all evening. Chad Allan, the lead singer, was hoarse and edgy. He screamed the lyrics as the others bashed away, and the tape that resulted sounded so bad it sounded good.

"There was this funny slapback echo on it," lead guitarist Randy Bachman recalls now, "and we thought, 'This is really cool. It sounds like Elvis.' So we sent it to Quality Records in Toronto and the guy said, 'This is a monster, but I don't want to put your name on it. The minute the stations know it's Canadian, they won't play it.' Nobody wanted a Canadian band back then. The British invasion was on. He said, 'Get a new name that's very British-sounding, and meanwhile I'm going to put out a white-label single saying, Guess Who? I want people to think it's one of these jam sessions with one of the Stones, and one of the Beatles, and some guys from other bands who had a party and were jamming in a basement.'"

The ruse worked. "'Shakin' All Over' by the Guess Who," as disc jockeys announced it, scored a hit across the country, riding the trend-setting CHUM Chart for 16 weeks, and peaking at number 4. It became the group's first success, but also burdened them with what Bachman calls a "stupid, utterly ridiculous" name. Three years of obscurity followed. Then in 1968, they caught the attention of a Toronto advertising producer, Jack Richardson, who had been the first person to hire pop stars to sing "Things go better with Coke," beginning with Canadian crooner Bobby Curtola. Now Richardson was proposing to record a mail-order rock album, available to buyers for $1.25 plus eight Coca-Cola bottle caps. He recruited the Guess Who and an Ottawa band, the Staccatos, cutting a record called *A Wild Pair* that sold nearly 85,000 copies, to that point the biggest success ever for a Canadian rock-band release.

Afterwards, Richardson and the Guess Who decided to work together permanently. The band liked Richardson for his enthusiasm and inventiveness, and Richardson liked the Guess Who, he once said, for "something you just couldn't put your finger on." Chad Allan had already left, replaced by Burton Cummings, a talented young singer and keyboard player. Bachman remained on lead guitar, Jim Kale on bass, and Garry Peterson on drums. Richardson bought their contract from Quality Records for $1,000, and in March 1968, he quit his advertising job to form the production company Nimbus 9.

The gamble paid off. Bachman and Cummings developed a knack for writing AM-radio hits, beginning with "These Eyes" in 1968, followed by "Laughing" and "Undun" the next year, and the overwhelming successes of 1970. Richardson produced all the early hits in New York and Chicago, and in 1973 plowed his share of the profits into building his own studio at Hazelton Avenue. He ran it there for the next six years, not only for the Guess Who, but also for other top international recording acts. At Nimbus 9, Alice Cooper recorded *Welcome to my Nightmare*, parts of Pink Floyd's *The Wall* were mixed, and Peter Gabriel recorded his first solo album. "John Denver, Ringo Starr, the Bay City Rollers – the list goes on and on," Richardson says.

"American Woman" remains the Guess Who's greatest hit. It also remains their greatest fluke, Bachman says. Its inspiration came by accident during a concert, and had luck not been with the band that night, the song might have disappeared altogether.

"We wrote it onstage at a hockey arena in Kitchener, Ontario," recalls Bachman, the key person in the song's genesis. "We had been touring the States for months, we were totally depressed, going through towns and not seeing any young men our age. They had all been drafted for Vietnam. It was a twilight zone. We'd go into towns and girls would come and touch us, and go, like, 'Real guys our own age,' because everybody was gone. Very depressing.

"And they tried to draft *us.* We had green cards, which means you are a resident alien, which means, 'What size are you? Forty-two tall? Here's a uniform and a rifle.' So we came back to Canada really fast.

"We arrived in Kitchener and the promoter said, 'We want you to play a three-hour jam.' And we said, 'Great,' because in the States we'd been playing shows with the Happenings and the Kingsmen, all kinds of bands, each playing about 20 or 30 minutes, and now we could play all our Beatles songs and instrumentals just like a normal high-school band.

"Then somewhere in the middle of the concert I broke a string. In those days I could afford a grand total of one guitar, so when I broke a string the band stopped playing. Burton said, 'We're going to take a break while Randy changes his string.' So I put on the new string, and as I was tuning it I started to play dah-dah-dah-dah, DAH, dah-dah. And the minute I started to play this, Peterson and Kale got so excited about something new happening that they came back onstage. We started jamming it as a three-piece, on and on. There were no words, just the riff, and we were soloing and everything.

"While all this is happening, Burton is out in the parking lot having a cigarette. He's talking to all his buddies, and he hears this music but he doesn't know it's us because he's never heard it before. He thinks they're playing a record. When you take a break they play records, right? So somebody goes up to him – he's leaning against a car – and says, 'Why aren't you up there playing?' He looks in the door, we're onstage, and he comes running up to join us.

"He played a flute solo, a piano solo, a harmonica solo. I was playing guitar. We were running out of solos and I said, 'Sing something,' and the first thing that came out of his mouth was 'American woman, stay away from me.' He sang that four times, we soloed some more, he sang the line again, and the song was over. There were no war machines, or ghetto scenes, or bright lights that hypnotize, just 'American woman, stay away from me.' But we thought, 'This is great.' We felt the excitement of the crowd, like a chemistry happening."

Jack Richardson, now a professor in audio production at Fanshawe College in London, Ontario, picks up the story. He says the song might have disappeared had a fan not taped the session with a portable cassette player, new at the time, and brought the tape backstage. The band members took the cassette to Richardson.

"They brought this tape into the studio at RCA in Chicago," he recalls, "and it was, I would say, about 10, maybe 12 minutes long. It consisted of about eight and a half minutes of Randy playing solo guitar, everybody wandering back onto the stage, and Burton coming up and singing, 'American woman, stay away from me.'

"They told me, 'Boy, the crowd just went crazy.' And I said, 'Well, unless we can send a crowd of 5,000 people out with every copy, the fact that you're going to play guitar for eight minutes, Randy, and Burton is going to sing "American woman, get away from me" – that isn't going to make much of a record.' So we all put our heads together, and developed the whole structure and lyrics right there in the studio."

"American Woman" topped the *Billboard* chart on May 9, 1970, coinciding with the growth of the U.S. antiwar movement. The timing was perfect. Private band resentments resulting from a tough road tour were transformed into popular political grievances, and the American woman became a clever political metaphor.

"We couldn't sing, 'Uncle Sam, stay away from me' or 'Richard Nixon, go screw yourself,'" Bachman says. "But 'American woman' had a certain ring to it, a certain phonetic beauty in the words. The American woman became the Statue of Liberty."

10

RPM Weekly

6 BRENTCLIFFE ROAD

Walt Grealis first got up on a high horse in 1947 when he joined the Royal Canadian Mounted Police. He served as a Mountie for five years, then joined the Toronto police department as a beat cop in Cabbagetown. After another five years, sick of breaking up street fights, he became by turns a sports director at a Bermuda hotel, a publicist for a Toronto beer company, and a promoter of one, and then another, Canadian record label.

Grealis next got up on a high horse in 1964. The domestic recording industry was a joke, he concluded. The studios were terrible, which meant that nobody bought the records, which meant that the labels made no money, which meant that the studios stayed terrible and that Canadian consumers continued to buy only American and European recordings. "We were hopelessly behind," Grealis still recalls with exasperation. "Most of the recording sessions were being done at primitive three-track facilities. Mastering in this country was near to impossible."

To break the cycle, Grealis quit his job and started a newsletter to harangue and encourage people into building a domestic music industry with local talent. He called the newsletter *RPM Weekly,* printing the first issue on a single page with a duplicating machine in his basement. "I knew nothing about publishing at all," he says, "and the only writing I had done was police reports."

With Mountie-like resolve, Grealis carried on. He wrote about the Allan Sisters, the Paupers, and Shirley Matthews, who had a song called "Big Town Boy." When a friend told him about Anne Murray in Halifax, he wrote about her, too. As sales and advertising grew, he built a small staff that included an acquaintance from the record business, Stan Klees, who helped expand the newsletter into a weekly trade magazine.

Soon they established the offices they still occupy, above a restaurant at 6 Brentcliffe Road, south of Eglinton Avenue East in Leaside. They began to issue special publications such as the *Canadian Music Industry Directory,* and the *RPM Starline Photo Album* of Canadian recording artists. They also printed a ballot in the magazine each year for readers to vote on their favorite acts, announcing the winners as

(Photo courtesy Walt Grealis)

Dressed in the scarlet tunic and broad-brimmed hat of the Royal Canadian Mounted Police, Walt Grealis sits on a high horse outside Regina, Saskatchewan, in 1948. With Mountie-like resolve, he went on to launch *RPM Weekly* in an effort to help build the domestic music industry.

recipients of the RPM Gold Leaf Awards, even though no actual awards existed.

"We just kept talking about the record business as if it was a giant industry, and it began to catch on," Grealis says. "We made everybody look important. We were building a star system and attempting to rid ourselves of the stigma that Canada was a country controlled by foreign branch offices."

The toughest people to win over were the radio stations' owners. In the 1960s, a record's success depended on radio play, and Canadian stations virtually refused to play Canadian records. The leading pop station, CHUM, promoted U.S. and British hits almost exclusively. The station ranked the hits on its own weekly CHUM Chart, which was distributed to other stations, record stores, and record-store customers. Canadian artists such as Bobby Curtola and the Guess Who made the charts because they recorded in the United States and had American hits, but artists who recorded in Canada barely stood a chance. As CHUM music director Bob McAdorey stated unapologetically in 1967, "Ninety percent of Canadian radio stations refuse to play an unproven record, whether it's from Czechoslovakia or Tillsonburg, Ontario. They don't feel any obligation to prove themselves heroes."

To break the stranglehold, Grealis began to promote the idea of a Canadian-content rule for radio. He wrote a 10-part series in his magazine about quotas in other countries, and calculated that up to $80 million in royalties was leaving Canada every year. He then sent copies of his articles to all five members of the Canadian Radio-Television Commission, established in 1968 under chairman Pierre Juneau.

Juneau proved open to Grealis's argument. The chairman began to speak boldly about "developing and encouraging Canadian talent," and in May 1970 he convened Canadian-content hearings in

Ottawa. When they ended, he announced the quotas that remain essentially unchanged to this day. He said that beginning on January 18, 1971, 30 percent of all songs played on Canadian radio must be written or performed by a Canadian, or recorded wholly in Canada.

Almost immediately, record companies began to invest in local artists, and almost immediately Grealis and Klees changed the name of the Gold Leaf Awards to the Juno Awards, in Juneau's honor. Klees also designed the metronome-style statuette that was first awarded in 1971 and is still in use. "Canadian-content legislation worked," Grealis still says unequivocally. "Without it, we wouldn't have the star system we have."

Grealis himself is now recognized as a fixture in the domestic music industry, hailed as the founder of the Juno Awards and the "Godfather of Can Con." In 1977, when *RPM Weekly* ceded administration of the Junos to the Canadian Academy of Recording Arts and Sciences, a new annual award was inaugurated in his honor. It is called the Walt Grealis Special Achievement Award for contribution to the industry.

11

Ontario Science Centre

770 DON MILLS ROAD

"Peace means no violence and everybody grooving," John Lennon told reporters at the Ontario Science Centre on December 17, 1969 – days before the 1960s ended.

Lennon and his wife, Yoko Ono, sat together in black clothes, chain-smoking French cigarettes, to announce that they would hold a Music and Peace Conference of the World the following July 3–5 northeast of the city at Mosport raceway. Speaking in quiet, peaceful tones, they said the festival would be bigger than Woodstock.

Plans are "still in the baby stage," Lennon said, "but we hope to set up such a good scene that we can take it to Russia and Czechoslovakia. I'll try to hustle [the other Beatles] out, and I'll even try to get Elvis. I'll try to get them all."

Admission to the festival would be free, he also said. A "peace vote" would be held, in which audience members would vote by secret ballot for peace or war. If the crowd chose peace, the festival would begin the year One A.P., meaning After Peace.

"If anybody thinks our campaign is naive, that's his opinion," Lennon said soothingly. "Let him do something for peace in the way he wants. We're artists. We do it in a way that suits us best."

That year had been a turbulent one for the Lennons. In March, they were married in Gibraltar, and began their world-peace campaign from their honeymoon bed in Amsterdam. In May, John was banned from entering the United States because of an earlier marijuana conviction in Britain. A bed-in planned for New York got switched to Montreal, which they reached via Toronto after authorities approved a provisional visa. In Scotland that summer, John drove his car off the road, injuring himself, Yoko, and her daughter, Kyoko; all of them needed stitches. In September, the couple returned to Toronto to play a one-day Rock and Roll Revival festival amid struggles with heroin addiction and conflicts with Paul, George, and Ringo. In October, Yoko suffered her second miscarriage in a year.

Now they were back in Toronto to renew the peace effort. They arrived on December 16, greeted by their own billboards saying "War is Over, if you want it – Happy Christmas from John and Yoko." Otherwise the mission began badly. Customs officials detained them for nearly four hours while searching their 26 pieces of luggage. Inexplicably, 12 copies of a live recording from their previous visit were seized. Afterwards a Rolls-Royce whisked the couple to the home of rockabilly singer Ronnie Hawkins, west of the city, where they were to stay the week. When a reporter and photographer from the *Toronto Star* tried to follow the car through the front gate, a security guard named Heavy Andrews punched the photographer in the face.

All week long the guests created havoc, Hawkins says. John left his pornographic lithographs where the Hawkins children could see them, and John and Yoko ran up a phone bill for thousands of dollars

– which, Hawkins says, they never paid. One night the visitors started to run a bath and fell asleep, causing the water to overflow and bring down the living-room ceiling. But the most terrifying moment came the next morning.

John Lennon and his wife, Yoko Ono, take their first snow-mobile ride on December 18, 1969, at a farm west of the city owned by rockabilly singer Ronnie Hawkins. The couple spent a week on the property planning the Music and Peace Conference of the World.

(Photo: Canapress)

"All of a sudden we heard this – sound," Hawkins says. "Someone was getting murdered, for sure. We jumped up and ran around. We didn't know what the hell it was. I was looking for guns and every other thing. But it was just Yoko. She was in her room singing."

Two days before Christmas, the Lennons travelled by train to Ottawa to meet Prime Minister Pierre Trudeau. A scheduled photo session turned into a 50-minute discussion. "If all politicians were like him, there would be world peace," John said on leaving. "It was a beautiful meeting," said Yoko. "He is beautiful."

One month later, however, plans for the peace festival fell apart. One of the organizers, Leonard Hollahan, announced that a bubbled hovercraft with no engine would transport the Lennons to Mosport. "The spaceship will be powered by the psychic energy waves coming from the crowd," he said. "Isn't that something?"

From England the Lennons dispatched a telegram in reaction stating, "We do not want to have anything to do with your festival. Please do not use our names or our ideas or symbols."

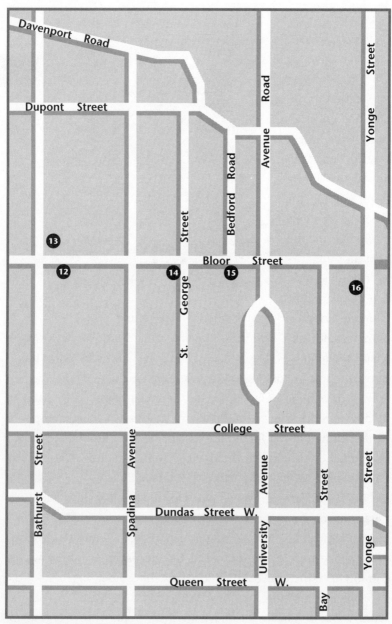

LEGEND: 12 – Lee's Palace; 13 – Bathurst Subway Station; 14 – Bata Shoe Museum;
15 – Varsity Stadium; 16 – The Incredible Record Store

12

Lee's Palace

529 BLOOR STREET WEST

Four years, almost to the day, before his shocking suicide, Kurt Cobain incited a bottle-throwing spree at Lee's Palace, bringing an early Nirvana concert to a chaotic finish. The date was April 16, 1990.

Almost nobody had heard of Cobain then. He grew up in the coastal logging town of Aberdeen, Washington, and moved to Seattle when he was nearly 20, in 1987, with his bass-guitarist friend, Krist Novoselic. A year later they formed Nirvana with drummer Chad Channing. They cut their first single, "Love Buzz," releasing only 1,000 copies on Sub Pop, the independent label that was also recording Mudhoney, Tad, Soundgarden, and other bands identified with what people were beginning to call the "Seattle sound" and what eventually became famous as "grunge."

For the next three years Nirvana lingered in semi-obscurity. They recorded an album, *Bleach;* they made appearances in Europe;

(Photo: John Goddard)

Distinguished by cartoon drawings by Toronto artist Runt, Lee's Palace is an eye-opening attraction on Bloor Street West. Kurt Cobain incited a beer-bottle-throwing spree here at an early Nirvana concert on April 16, 1990.

Dave Grohl replaced Channing on drums. Then they made their move. They jumped to a major label, Geffen, and in 1991 released their second album, *Nevermind,* which shot to number 1 on the U.S. and Canadian charts, selling 4 million copies in six months in the United States alone. Suddenly, Nirvana was huge. With their crashing instruments and throat-searing vocals on hits such as "Smells Like Teen Spirit" and "Come As You Are," the band leapt to the forefront of the raw, underground neo-punk movement from the Pacific Northwest.

Nirvana toured Australia, New Zealand, Europe, and Japan. They continued to write and record. For Cobain, however, the pressure grew unbearable. His inarticulate lyrics and often-volatile stage persona masked what friends described as a shy, sensitive personality. For solace he turned to heroin, and to Courtney Love, the unstable lead singer of Hole. They got married and had a daughter, and less than two years later – on April 5, 1994 – Cobain put a shotgun barrel between his teeth and pulled the trigger. He was 27 years old.

The Lee's Palace date came after *Bleach* but well before *Nevermind,* when Cobain, Novoselic, and Channing were touring unaccompanied for seven weeks in a van. Their local contact was Elliott Lefko, a promoter who books most of the acts at Lee's Palace, a medium-sized club on the south side of Bloor Street, east of Bathurst, distinguished by cartoon drawings by the local artist Runt.

Another contact was Tim Perlich, a rock reporter for the local entertainment weekly *Now*. Perlich had interviewed the band by phone a few days earlier, and although he had already filed his story, he went to the show, expecting it to be lively. He was not disappointed. The story of what happened that night comes from him.

"The show was pretty well attended," Perlich begins. "It was a Monday night and there were at least 200 people there, but I guess Cobain was a bit upset that nobody was getting up on the floor and jumping around. A lot of people were sitting at tables, and this sort of upset or offended him. He had never been to Toronto before, so I guess he didn't really know how to react to standoffish Toronto audiences, which they typically are. So he got down off the stage and started wandering around. This was fairly late in the show. His guitar was still plugged in, he was still playing, and he was sort of glaring and growling at people. He was walking right up to people's tables and pushing his guitar in their face and stuff.

(Photo: Canapress)

"Then he picked up a beer bottle and threw it at the back wall. He snatched it right off one of the tables – beer was spilling out of it – and he threw it right over Chad Channing's head at the big

Kurt Cobain of Nirvana demonstrates the intense stage persona he became known for, while performing in 1993, just months before committing suicide on April 5, 1994.

plaster wall where it says 'Lee's Palace' behind the band. Beer and glass just splattered everywhere. I had never seen anything like this in a Toronto club, and I guess nobody else had either.

"A couple of seconds elapsed, and suddenly everyone got the idea that this was the thing to do. Everybody started throwing beer bottles at the back wall at Lee's. There were 30, 40, 50 bottles smashing against the wall, and when Elliott saw what was happening, he started to worry about the damage that was being done, or might be done if people continued to do this.

"So Elliott, who is sort of a shy personality, not a really robust character or an imposing figure at all, just a normal, reedy sort of guy with glasses, jumped up onstage and started waving his arms and shouting, 'Stop, stop, everybody stop,' while the band was finishing off their song. Bottles were whizzing by his head. He was shaking. There was broken glass everywhere, and at this point Krist Novoselic, the bassist, who rarely wears shoes onstage, or didn't at that point – maybe he does now – jumped on top of his bass cabinet to avoid getting his feet cut on the glass.

"He was a bit drunk, and he was standing on top of his bass amp, almost to the ceiling. He's about six-six or six-seven, so he's way, way up in the sky. And somebody throws a bottle. I was off to the side watching all this unfold. I watched this bottle tumble end over end through the air and catch Krist right on the bridge of the nose. He teetered back and fell to the stage on his ass. Then Kurt and Chad knocked over the drum kit and that was the end of the show.

"I had interviewed them, so I decided to go back and say hello. The backstage area is actually beside the stage, so everybody is standing around looking at all the glass and shaking their heads. We're looking at all this mess, and the friend I was with, Craig, says, 'Check this out,' and he points to the wall. Embedded in the wall is a beer bottle, neck-deep in the plaster. It was like a *Twilight Zone* episode, when somebody flips a coin and it lands on its edge or something. Whenever we talk about that gig now, we say, 'Do you remember the bottle?' As if we could forget. That kind of thing really sticks in your mind. Sometimes we just refer to it as 'The Bottle.'

"Anyway, we're backstage and Elliott tells me that the guys didn't have any place to sleep. Elliott was working on a low budget. He had a really small apartment, and sometimes when he had somebody else staying with him, he would ask me to put someone up. And I said, 'Yeah, no problem, really.' Other bands had stayed at my place before – other Sub Pop bands, actually. Members of Tad, Mudhoney. Some people were starting to call my place the Sub Pop Hotel, because of all these Sub Pop bands staying there.

"We stayed up quite late that night talking. I remember I didn't have any bread left, and Kurt was eating peanut butter out of the jar with a spoon. I asked him about 'Love Buzz.' For a long time I have been a big fan of Dutch rock music from the sixties, and Dutch punk music, and I had Nirvana's first single, 'Love Buzz,' which was a cover of the B side of a single by the Shocking Blue. They were a Dutch group that had a hit in 1969 with 'Venus,' but their other material was not well known at all. So I asked Kurt where he got the song. I thought maybe he was a collector of Dutch music as well, maybe he had a lot of that kind of stuff. But he said, 'No, I didn't even really know who the group was. This guy who used to live next door to us had all these rock records from the sixties, and he played it for me.' I don't think he even knew it was a Shocking Blue song, or that they were Dutch, or cared, really. He just thought it was a cool song.

"Kurt filled me in on a lot of things about his childhood, and the people that he knew and hung around with, and where he worked and stuff like that. He said he spent a lot of time in his bedroom, and once worked at the perfume counter at the local Kmart. I started thinking that the place he was describing sounded a lot like *Twin Peaks,* which I had been watching on TV. There had been about six episodes at that point, so I said, 'Well, you must be really digging *Twin Peaks.*' And he said, 'What's that?'

"I said, 'It's the David Lynch series that just started up.' And he said, 'We haven't been watching any TV because we've been on the road and in the studio.' He knew who David Lynch was, of course, but he didn't know anything about *Twin Peaks,* so I said, 'Well, you've got to check this out, because Twin Peaks is like the place where you grew up.'

"My room-mate and I had taped all the episodes. We had them all back to back on videotape, so I stuck one on and said, 'Check this out, but I'm going to sleep.' By this time it's 3 a.m. or something. I just left them like that.

"Then at around, I don't know, five in the morning, I got up for a glass of water and I heard some noise. The lights were still on, and they were all still up watching *Twin Peaks.* They were watching every single episode. Their eyes were glued to the screen, like zombies. They were all just speechless, watching all the episodes about this lumbering town in the northwest, with small-town mores, just like Aberdeen. They really dug it, and from that point on I became known as the *Twin Peaks* guy. In all my subsequent meetings with Kurt and Krist, whenever I saw them or talked to them on the phone, they would say, 'Oh, it's the *Twin Peaks* guy.'

"For instance, about a week before *Nevermind* came out, they came back to Toronto [on September 24, 1991] to start another tour. They did sort of a showcase gig at the Opera House [at 735 Queen Street East]. I saw Krist out front, and he said, 'Come on back, Kurt would probably like to say hi.' I went back, and Krist said, 'Hey Kurt, check it out, the *Twin Peaks* guy.'

"It was kind of funny, but they were like that – really nice guys. Kurt Cobain was just like a regular guy. He wasn't like a rock star. At that time these guys weren't well known at all. They were just guys from a small town in the northwest who had no idea that they were going to become popular, and had no interest, really, in becoming huge stars.

"I never imagined Nirvana ever becoming as popular as they did. I don't think anybody would have predicted that. I imagined them selling maybe 20,000 copies of a record. They had a good pop sensibility, and they could reach a lot of people if they got the right exposure. But who would have thought MTV would get behind them the way they did, and *Spin,* and *Rolling Stone,* and all these different machines that fell into place? They were the right band for the moment. They had the right sound for what people wanted to hear, and it all clicked."

13

Bathurst Subway Station

BATHURST AND BLOOR STREETS

Bathurst subway station is no fun in February, says Paul Dakota, a founding member with Greg McConnell of the Lost Dakotas street band. Cold winds blow down from the bus bay to where the duo once played for hours at a time, their picking fingers stiffening slowly into uselessness. "February is crazy at Bathurst," Dakota says, "but then February is nuts anywhere."

Dakota and McConnell first gained a following aboveground, at the corner of Yonge and Dundas Streets. They called themselves simply the Dakotas then. All through the summer of 1990, they sang together next to a cardboard cactus for six or seven hours a day, Dakota playing acoustic guitar, McConnell playing standup bass. When their material wore thin, they took breaks at the nearby World's Biggest Bookstore, at 20 Edward Street, scribbling lyrics and chord changes from songbooks in the upstairs music section.

"Everything we ever listened to started coming out," Dakota says. They played Hank Williams alongside AC/DC, and Creedence Clearwater Revival back to back with the Sex Pistols. Gradually they built a repertoire of 300 songs.

That August they entered the subway auditions. Once a year, the Toronto Transit Commission holds a competition for buskers who wish to play for change in the subway system. The privilege is highly regulated. Three judges from established musical societies assess 200 or more applicants for stage presence, entertainment value, and musical ability. Positions go to the top 75 acts. Winners pay $100 per person for a busking licence and join a roster that circulates them through 25 designated locations in three time slots over the next calendar year.

The Dakotas took the top score. "Number 1 ranking at the 1991 subway auditions" became their claim to fame, and their bright-green cactus soon became a familiar sight at Bathurst station as the duo negotiated with other buskers to keep the location. A regular spot gained them a core audience. They made a tape and sold 1,200 copies to passers-by. They added a drummer and a second guitarist, and changed their name to the Lost Dakotas – "because it sounded better," Dakota says. They never made it big, but by the time their licence expired, they had recorded their first independent CD. *Last Train to Kipling,* they called it, after the westernmost station on the Bloor Street line.

14

Bata Shoe Museum

327 BLOOR STREET WEST

"Pop culture reigns," says Jonathan Walford, a curator at the Bata Shoe Museum, the only footwear museum in North America. "We paid more money for Elton John's boots from the 1970s than for a pair of Egyptian sandals from 2500 BC. And the boots attract more attention."

Walford is talking about one of the more eye-popping exhibits from a collection of 8,500 or so items owned by the Thomas and Sonja Bata shoe-manufacturing family. Sonja began accumulating the shoes on foreign travels soon after her marriage to the company chairman in 1946. At first, she acquired with an eye to unusual features. Later, she purchased with a view to how shoes reflect society and culture. In 1996, she opened the museum. Financed entirely by family money and designed by Raymond Moriyama, it stands at Bloor and St. George Streets like an outsize shoebox, its canted copper roof suggesting a lid casually left askew.

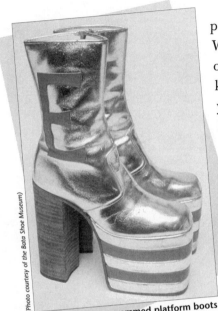

(Photo courtesy of the Bata Shoe Museum)

Elton John's monogrammed platform boots from 1972 are one of the biggest attractions at the Bata Shoe Museum. They also cost the museum more to buy than a pair of Egyptian sandals from 2500 BC.

"You can tell a lot about people by their footwear," says Walford of the collection's serious ethnological purpose. "You know when you're a kid, and you don't bother untying your laces? You slide your shoes on your feet and break down the backs, and your mum yells at you? Well, in Morocco wearing shoes with the backs broken down was often a status symbol. It meant you were removing your shoes for prayers several times a day at the mosque."

Ethnological insight edifies the displays; the footwear of the rich and famous draws the crowds. On the basement level, beyond some thirteenth-century foot armor and Hausa camel-riding gear, a spiral staircase ascends to a featured exhibit called Star Turns. At front row centre lie the prized items: the outrageous silver-and-red platform boots from 1973 that helped establish Elton John as Britain's king of glitter rock. The letters "E" and "J" appear in red capitals at the back of either heel.

"We paid about $12,000 for them," Walford says, "one of the best investments we've ever made. First of all, there is a photograph of Elton John wearing them. Also, they appear on the 1988 *Reg Strikes Back* album. Plus, they are famous as the ones he once got stopped for in Los Angeles. He had to put all his shoes through the X-ray machine because the customs officials thought they might contain contraband."

Sometimes, instead of the silver-and-red boots, a pair of solid-grey ones go on display, Walford says. "We have two pairs from Elton John – one for the museum and one for special exhibitions in other places."

Walford runs through other items of pop-music interest.

"The red ballet slippers that Kate Bush wore on the cover of her 1993 *Red Shoes* album.

"David Bowie's running shoes from the Serious Moonlight tour, 1984. The back of one says 'Serious,' and the back of the other says 'Moonlight.'

"Elvis Presley's blue-and-white patent-leather loafers from the early 1970s. We also have the shirt that he wore with them.

"A single Beatle boot from John Lennon. We got it at auction in England, through a woman who had known the Beatles road manager and had begged for a memento [after a concert at Birmingham in 1965]. Lennon had a pair of boots that were worn out and that he was about to throw away. I don't know if the woman got both or just the one, but only one went to auction.

"Buddy Holly's winkle-pickers. A winkle is a snail, and the picker is that little tool you use to get the snail out of its shell, so calling them winkle-pickers is sort of making fun of the pointed toes. These are brown suede monk-strapped loafers, which means that the buckle is on the side rather than dead centre. We got them from an estate auction of his wife. Presumably they were in his wardrobe when he died [in an air crash with Ritchie Valens and the Big Bopper in February 1959].

"And a very unlikely pair of extremely sexy high-heeled evening shoes from Anne Murray, with silver sparkles, and an actually boring pair of runners from Cher. She maybe should have the sexy ones, but she's also into the fitness thing."

15

Varsity
Stadium

277 BLOOR STREET WEST

John Brower was desperate. He was 23 years old and the promoter of what he called the Toronto Rock and Roll Revival show. It was scheduled for Varsity Stadium on September 13, 1969, starring Chuck Berry, Jerry Lee Lewis, Fats Domino, Gene Vincent, Bo Diddley, Little Richard, and the Doors. But with three days to go, Brower had sold only 800 of his 20,000 tickets. Frantic for publicity, he phoned to offer John Lennon free seats to attend.

It was the longest of long shots. Brower tailored his pitch to Lennon's love of early rock-and-roll acts, aware that Gene Vincent, particularly, had been an early Lennon idol. Brower also placed hope in Lennon's new accessibility. The previous spring, Lennon and Yoko Ono had held their famous press conferences for world peace from their honeymoon bed at the Amsterdam Hilton. They had followed with a similar event at the Queen Elizabeth Hotel in

Montreal, using an impromptu chorus of visitors to help record "Give Peace a Chance." Unknown to Brower, Lennon was also fighting with Paul McCartney and looking for a way to go it alone. Lennon said he would come to the concert if he could play.

Brower could hardly believe his ears. No Beatle had ever performed solo. The Beatles as a group had not played a concert for three years, not counting their rooftop performance at their London headquarters that January for the film *Let It Be*. As Lennon threw a band together and scrambled for the airport, Brower announced Lennon's imminent arrival. The concert sold out almost instantly.

On the big day, Brower arranged for 80 members of the outlaw Vagabond biker club to escort the car bearing Lennon and his entourage from the airport, like a scene from *The Wild One*. With Lennon were Yoko Ono, a drummer name Alan White from the British band Yes, bass player Klaus Voormann, who had known the Beatles since their early Hamburg days, and guitarist Eric Clapton. Most were not in great shape. On the ride over, Lennon and Clapton had gone into heroin withdrawal and held their only rehearsal on unamplified electric guitars between pauses to throw up in the airplane's washroom. At the stadium, Lennon and Ono scored enough cocaine to pull themselves together, but Clapton was sick again backstage and had to be roused to consciousness before going on.

Their performance proved less than spectacular. Lennon introduced the set by walking to the microphone in a fragile way and saying, "We're just going to do numbers that we know, you know, because we've never played together before." He introduced the musicians as the Plastic Ono Band, and kicked off with the early Carl Perkins hit "Blue Suede Shoes." The band followed with "Money," "Dizzy Miss Lizzy," the Lennon composition "Yer Blues," and a new song Lennon had written with Ono called "Cold Turkey."

"We've never done this number before, so best of luck," Lennon said as Ono held lyric sheets for him to sing from. The set finished with a rousing version of "Give Peace a Chance," after which Lennon announced, "Now Yoko's going to do her thing all over you."

Ono had spent much of her time onstage inside a white canvas bag making noises like rewind tape chatter. Now she threw herself into a number called "Don't Worry, Kyoko (Mummy's Only Looking for a Hand in the Snow)." For 20 minutes she howled and shrieked against a background of guitar feedback created when Lennon, Clapton, and Voormann rested their guitars against live amplifiers.

"Yoko's unmusical wails and whoops almost drove the crowd insane with boredom," the *Toronto Star* reported afterwards. Ono's voice "stretched into endless tedium, full of cries from hell, piercing, evil shrieks, tiny sounds that reminded you of a finger nail scratching across a blackboard," the reports said. Lennon "merely stood with his hands in his pockets looking like a man waiting for a very late streetcar."

In early January 1970, the live album *Plastic Ono Band: Live Peace in Toronto* entered the U.S. charts. It peaked at number 10 for two weeks in February, and by mid-March had racked up sales of more than $1 million. On April 10, the Beatles announced that they had disbanded.

16

The Incredible Record Store

778 YONGE STREET

Jonathon Lipsin is a walking rebuttal to the adage that "if you can remember the sixties, you weren't really there." Lipsin was there – *and* he remembers. In the callowness of his youth, he wandered Forrest Gump–like through seminal events of the period, picking up odd jobs from celebrated revolutionaries and now-fabled musicians.

"It was the greatest of all times," he says.

For 15 years, until recently, Lipsin owned and operated the Incredible Record Store, a second-floor walkup on Yonge Street south of Bloor, specializing in keeping the spirit of the late 1960s and early 1970s alive. The street entrance led to a steep staircase plastered with posters mostly of San Francisco–area bands and of Jimi Hendrix, Janis Joplin, and Jim Morrison in their prime. At the top of the stairs, the room opened to a jumble of wooden bins stuffed with used records, many selling for as little as $2 each. The aisles were narrow, and the walls covered with memorabilia – some for sale, some for sale only theoretically. A large black-and-white photograph of 1950s rocker Bill Haley backstage at Maple Leaf Gardens was priced at $250. An autographed guitar played by Randy Bachman in his Guess Who and Bachman-Turner Overdrive days carried a tag of $10,000, plus the stipulation that it remain in Canada as "a national treasure."

"I sell records and CDs, but essentially I'm a curator," Lipsin often says. He is a compact man with short ginger hair, a trim beard, and an intensity that makes it easy to imagine him as a teenager exploring the world at a time of unprecedented opportunity and freedom. But the winds of conservatism are now blowing, he says. A slow retail economy hasn't helped. Reluctantly, in late 1996, he made vague plans to relocate somewhere in California.

"There is a danger of culture being lost," he says of his biggest regret in closing. "A lot of kids these days don't know anything about the sixties. I've met kids who hate the Beatles. They don't know John Lennon. They know *Rolling Stone* magazine only as a glossy. The Incredible Record Store offered a cultural link."

Lipsin's own connection to 1960s counter-culture began in Montreal, where he grew up. He moved from his parents' house to a downtown commune, where he slept in a sleeping bag on the floor, grew his hair into a gigantic afro, and began hitchhiking to New York and elsewhere seeking to become part of a larger scene. The year was 1969. Lipsin was 15.

Once, he crashed in Greenwich Village with Tuli Kupferberg, the former Beat poet turned iconoclastic musician with the Fugs, who played, as Lipsin puts it, for "weddings, bar mitzvahs, and revolutions." Allen Ginsberg lived next door, and Lipsin felt in the thick of things. He moved into a nearby loft, where he erected a pup tent for himself next to a space serving as offices for the Underground Press Syndicate and for Abbie Hoffman's and Jerry Rubin's Youth International Party – the Yippies. Hoffman at the time was also writing his anarchistic Yippie manifesto, *Steal This Book*, and Lipsin contributed items on subjects such as panhandling and sneaking free rides on airplanes, activities he never actually attempted himself.

Eventually, radical politics soured for Lipsin. In the summer of 1970, a few weeks shy of his seventeenth birthday, he left for California. "I hitchhiked out of New York looking for a place in the country to write," he recalls. "Along the way, I got a ride with two other people, who offered the driver a little grass if he would take us to Bolinas. Bolinas is a little town north of San Francisco. We got there, and we all went into this little shack on the beach to smoke the grass. I got very wrecked and I walked – I stumbled – out to the beach, and there were people riding horses, people naked, people playing guitars, hippies, it was paradise, incredible. I just stumbled around going, 'Where have I landed?' And Grace Slick comes out of a house on the beach and says, 'What a great day!'"

For a while, Lipsin stayed in Bolinas, and drifted from there to neighboring Stinson Beach. Janis Joplin's ashes were sprinkled from a plane overhead that fall, and Lipsin smoked several memorial joints to her, on a hill with people who had known her. Soon afterwards, he began to mix with Jerry Garcia and the Grateful Dead.

"Stinson Beach was 500 people then," he says. "The Dead lived there. Officially the Dead were five guys, but they had an extended family of probably 100 people doing various things, and I ended up going to their parties and hanging out with them. Then one day I saw Garcia on the street. Everybody always called him Garcia, by the way, never Jerry. Not out of disrespect – it was just Garcia. I walked up to him and said, 'I'd like to get a job gardening and doing odd jobs.' And he said, 'Okay.' Simple as that. And for the next couple of years, I was like part of the family."

As a gardener, Lipsin admits to no special qualifications. "I didn't even know what I was doing," he says. On the other hand, his clients' standards were not high. "It was pretty loose and easy." Extended-family members lived in about a dozen ramshackle hilltop houses, and Lipsin earned his keep by watering lawns, cutting shrubs, and making general repairs.

"I used to take lunch breaks in the archives room," he recalls, "where the Dead kept all their tapes and slides from about 1964 to 1967. Nowadays kids would go crazy to get their hands in there, but back then it was no big deal. It was just part of the scene."

Afterwards, Lipsin drifted to Vancouver and to Europe. He served as a soldier in the Israeli army, then as a record promoter in Toronto, launching *One Elephant/Deux Éléphants,* the first children's album by Sharon, Lois and Bram, which sold 100,000 copies in seven months and won a Juno award.

Between jobs in 1983, Lipsin paused to reflect. "Life is short," he remembers telling himself. "If I could do anything I wanted, what would I do?" His answer was to open the record store, which he also – because of his special connection – designated "the Grateful Dead Headquarters of Canada." He devoted prime shelf space to such items as Jerry Gar-Chia Pets and commissioned hand-sewn

(Photo courtesy Jonathon Lipsin)

Jonathon Lipsin sports one of the world's greatest afros during his California days spent with the Grateful Dead. "I just stumbled around going, 'Where have I landed?'" he says of his arrival there in 1970.

dolls of all the band members. He sold a Dead trivia game, Dead magazines, a Deadbase discography guide, up to 50 CDs not found in other music stores – none of them bootlegs – and hundreds of Dead-related stickers, patches, and T-shirts. Pictures of Lipsin himself from his Dead days sometimes adorned the walls, showing his exposed chest and magnificent afro.

Another feature of the store became a wooden museum case displaying some of his most prized mementos. "John Lennon's guitar pick from 1965," Lipsin says, of a reddish-brown triangle with the word "Fender" in white lettering mostly worn away. "A woman came in one day and said, 'My therapist told me to get rid of my memories – here.'" He mentions other items, including a note from Leonard Cohen dated Thursday, June 3, 1993, and saying, "This is the greatest record store in Canada." He has 45-rpm singles of "Love Me Do" and "P.S. I Love You," released by the Beatles before Ringo joined. In the same case stood a copy of John and Yoko's *Wedding Album,* showing the couple naked on the cover, and an original banned cover of the Beatles *"Yesterday" … and Today* album from 1966, showing the Fab Four in bloody butcher's smocks holding dismembered dolls.

"The rarest record cover in rock history," Lipsin says. "A few years back, one of them sold at Sotheby's for $10,000. I've had offers – really good offers – but I'd rather have the cover."

In-store displays changed from time to time depending on his mood, Lipsin says, but one that he left on the wall for a long time was a tribute to the Woodstock music festival on its twenty-fifth anniversary. In August 1969, one week before his sixteenth birthday, Lipsin tried twice to get there.

"My hair was three feet long, I wasn't wearing a shirt, and they refused me at the border," he recalls of the first attempt. On his second try, hair slicked down with Brylcreem and tucked under a cap, he made it across.

"Woodstock wasn't just a festival," he says, his voice suddenly rising. "Woodstock went way beyond a festival. At Woodstock, we realized how strong we were. We realized that we could end the war in Vietnam. We realized that we could change the way we looked, the way we worked, the way we played. We realized that we could create our own rules, and do whatever we wanted to do. Everything important I've ever learned, I learned at Woodstock. Everything else was just commentary."

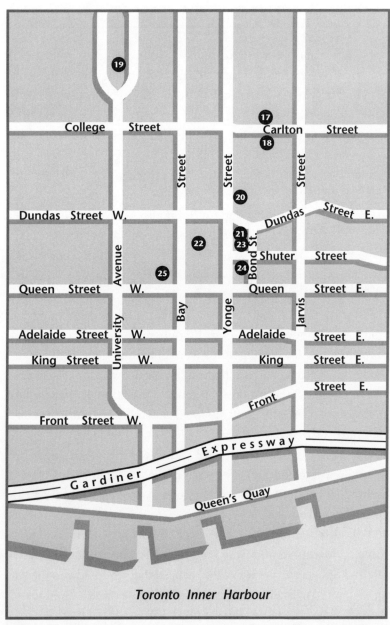

LEGEND: 17 – Maple Leaf Gardens; 18 – The Golden Griddle; 19 – Office of the Premier; 20 – Sam the Record Man; 21 – The Hard Rock Café (Friar's Tavern); 22 – Church of the Holy Trinity; 23 – St. Michael's Choir School; 24 – Massey Hall; 25 – Nathan Phillips Square

17

Maple Leaf Gardens

60 CARLTON STREET

Maple Leaf Gardens ranks as one of the most famous buildings in the country, drawing tourists for decades to the warm glow of its yellow-brick exterior. Built in five and a half months during the Great Depression, it opened on November 12, 1931, for a hockey game between the Toronto Maple Leafs and the Chicago Black Hawks. The Hawks won 2–1, but that season the Leafs won the Stanley Cup.

The Gardens remains first and foremost a hockey arena. Not a single rock-music memento adorns the Gardens' walls. Large color photographs of Madonna and Mick Jagger might be good enough for the SkyDome, home of baseball's Blue Jays, but at the Gardens, only team photos and portraits of individual players qualify. Never mind that Bill Haley and the Comets ushered rock and roll into Toronto with "Rock Around the Clock" there on April 30, 1956.

Never mind that Elvis Presley made his only career appearance in Toronto at the Gardens for two shows on April 2, 1957, to the largest crowd he had ever before seen. Never mind that when tickets to the first Beatles concert there went on sale at the same time as seats to the 1964 Stanley Cup playoffs, former hockey great Charlie Conacher phoned to say, "Forget the Leafs – get me some Beatles tickets." On the Gardens' walls, about the only concession to a world outside hockey is a black-and-white photo of Bob Hope.

The message is not lost on musicians. In 1962, Chubby Checker paid tribute to the great game by performing "The Twist" in a Leafs hockey sweater borrowed from the dressing room. He started a craze – many rock stars after him donned Leafs sweaters as well, including Elton John, the Bee Gees, ABBA, and Pete Townshend of the Who. One performer extended the tribute further, asking to skate on the Gardens' ice with the Maple Leafs themselves. That performer was Tiny Tim.

(Photo: Frank Prazak, courtesy of the Hard Rock Café Canada)

Variously described as sounding like Eleanor Roosevelt and looking like Joan Baez without sleep, Tiny Tim raises his arms to cheer the Toronto Maple Leafs in early 1968. "One of my dreams would be to live next to Maple Leaf Gardens and see every game there," he once said.

Tim has been variously described as sounding like Eleanor Roosevelt and looking like Joan Baez after a week without sleep. He stood tall and gangly, with a large nose and long scraggly hair, and although he was obsessively clean – often showering four times a day – people often took him for a dirty hippie. He was perceived as a novelty act, specializing in show tunes dating to the 1920s, which he sang in a cracked falsetto while playing the ukulele. Stardom came in 1968, when he was 43, with a Top 10 single, "Tip-Toe Thru' the Tulips with Me." Music was his first love; hockey and baseball came a close second.

"People used to throw things at me," he once said of his early nightclub days in New York's Greenwich Village. "But I was like [Leafs goalie] Mr. Terry Sawchuk. I was in the nets. I had my ukulele for a goalie stick and I used to bat away the pucks just as they were shot at me."

Tim grew up as Herbert Khaury in Brooklyn, New York, supporting baseball's Brooklyn Dodgers. He discovered hockey in 1943, when looking for something to cheer about in the off-season. He chose the Maple Leafs as his favorite team, he said, "because the maple leaf seemed close to nature and I like maple syrup. Also the word 'Toronto' has a nice ring to it."

In 1945, his commitment to hockey deepened when he found the CBC hockey broadcasts on his radio dial. As he recalled in 1968 for Patrick Nagle of *Weekend Magazine,* "I said to myself, 'Wow! It's a miracle. I'm in *Hockey Night in Canada.*'" He later subscribed to *Hockey News,* and sent away for an official Maple Leafs calendar. "I once bought an official hockey puck and carried it around with me all the time," he also said. "I used to bounce it off the wall of my room and catch it and pretend I had made a great save off the stick of Mr. Bobby Hull."

As his passion grew, Tim began to attend Leafs games when they played against the New York Rangers at Madison Square Garden. He would wear white face powder and lipstick to the games so that he could go straight to the club stage afterwards. Fans yelled at him and once poured beer over him, partly because he looked so weird, but also because he cheered so loudly for the Leafs.

"One of my dreams would be to live next to Maple Leaf Gardens and see every game there," he told Nagle at *Weekend*. "I just love sitting right behind the glass. It makes me feel like I'm part of the game. I cherish the sights and sounds of it, the flash of the skates on the ice. And I'm as close as can be to the goalie. Deep down I'm really a goalie at heart. One of my dreams would be to put on the goalie pads some day and have someone shoot at me. Someone like Mr. [Jean] Béliveau or Mr. Bobby Hull. It would be such a thrill. Or Mr. Tim Horton. Those shots go a hundred miles an hour."

Tim never put on goalie pads, but in the spring of 1969 he came close to realizing the fantasy. While in Toronto for a show, he arranged to skate with the Leafs at the Gardens.

"They put him on a pair of skates, but he couldn't stand up," recalls Jim McKenny, a popular Leafs defenceman at the time, and now an equally popular sportscaster on CITY-TV.

"I was one of the guys that held him up," McKenny says not unkindly. "Me and Shakey [Mike] Walton. The old guys on the team, Bobby Baun and Allan Stanley and some of those guys, wouldn't touch him. They said they thought he might have lice or something. But Shakey grabbed me. He says, 'Come on – we'll get some ink here, let's go help him out.' There was a photographer there, and we'd do anything to get our picture in the paper.

"And I remember hanging on to him," McKenny continues. "He was like a jelly roll. He had no muscle or anything. But I liked him. He was okay – him and Miss Vicky."

Miss Vicky was Victoria Budinger. On December 17, 1969, in his most famous public performance ever, Tiny Tim married her live on *The Tonight Show,* starring Johnny Carson, before a viewing audience of 40 million people.

18 The Golden Griddle

45 CARLTON STREET

Ashley MacIsaac spent the early hours of his twentieth birthday watching television at the Golden Griddle pancake house on Carlton Street, smack opposite Maple Leaf Gardens. MacIsaac likes watching television. "I watch probably eight to 10 hours of TV a day," he says. He also likes to smoke, which helps explain why at around 5 a.m. on February 24, 1995, after working into the night, he found himself in the rear smoking section of a restaurant looking up at a television set mounted near the ceiling. The set was tuned to TVOntario, showing a science program called *The Discovery of Radioactivity: Properties of Vectral Rays and Natural Transmutations.*

"It was one hour long," MacIsaac says, "and by the end of it I had relearned how to factor my numbers to the point of being able to make a nuclear reactor. So it was a good program."

(Photo: Derek Shapton, A&M Records)

"I watch probably eight to 10 hours of TV a day," says rock fiddler Ashley MacIsaac, who possesses what he calls "dimensional vision." His mind jumps from thought to thought, or dimension to dimension — "like Keith Richards."

Natural Transmutations might have made a good title for the Celtic fiddle album he was recording at the time, later released as *Hi™ How Are You Today?* MacIsaac possesses what he calls "dimensional vision," meaning that his mind jumps from thought to thought, or dimension to dimension — sion, picking up and combining information – "like Keith Richards."

"I didn't have any set of intentions," he says of starting the album that would alienate some of his earlier fans, but bring him glory on the rock scene. "Some of the stuff just came up as I was meeting different musicians and producers, and watching different TV shows."

At heart MacIsaac is a traditionalist. He grew up in the town of Creignish, on Cape Breton Island, Nova Scotia, listening to a style of music brought by Catholic Scots from the Highlands in the late 1700s. It is a clean, energetic style, not schmaltzy or sentimental, and nothing like "Danny Boy" rendered in fat, lugubrious tones. From a young age he learned to step-dance to it; at 8 he started playing it on the fiddle; at 13 he began to travel with other East Coast musicians to perform for Celtic-music audiences from Massachusetts to California, stopping occasionally in Toronto to entertain such groups as the Cape Breton Club.

At 16, he made his New York connection. JoAnne Akalaitis, a New York theatre director, heard him at a Cape Breton square dance when she was on vacation, and hired him for five months to perform in a show. Through her, MacIsaac met Philip Glass, the avant-garde composer; and through him, MacIsaac met Paul Simon, who invited MacIsaac onstage with him at Carnegie Hall.

"The following week I went to Newfoundland for the East Coast Music Awards, and the buzz was there," MacIsaac recalls of a sudden interest in him. "I did a 20-minute set. I played 10 minutes of traditional stuff and finished with 'Stayin' Alive,' which was the only dance song I knew, and when the record-company agents heard it, they all went, 'Wow, we can sell this guy – he's a freak.'"

Choice of music aside, MacIsaac also got noticed for his stage antics. Most Cape Breton fiddlers let the music speak for itself; MacIsaac performs recklessly, often at breakneck speed. He pitches forward at the waist, pumps his bowing arm high in the air, and stomps time on the floorboards in black army boots. Often, he wears a kilt.

A&M Records signed him and brought him to Toronto. They booked him into his favorite Toronto hotel, the Essex Park near Maple Leaf Gardens, and encouraged him to think about the kind of record he might want to make. At first, he said he wanted to make a dance record. He had liked the New York dance clubs, he said, but the A&M people said that dance music changes all the time. Fads come and go. They suggested he take more of a rock approach, which led him to try putting traditional fiddle tunes to a backbeat. "I didn't want it to sound like a typical Celtic-rock album," he says.

Soon the transmutations began. When he wasn't watching television, MacIsaac went out to meet local musicians, including guitarist Gordie Johnson of Big Sugar, keyboard player Chris Brown of the

Bourbon Tabernacle Choir, and drummer Graeme Kirkland, best known for his solo performances at downtown street corners bashing plastic buckets. All three artists ended up on the album, along with various classical musicians, two bass guitarists, a bagpipe player, and a traditional spoon tapper. After several months, MacIsaac completed 13 tracks. They ranged from the lilting "MacDougall's Pride" to the grating "The Devil in the Kitchen" to a sweet ballad called "Sleepy Maggie" – the latter played by MacIsaac on fiddle and sung in Gaelic by Cape Breton vocalist Mary Jane Lamond, backed by an electric rock band.

MacIsaac went from playing union halls and community centres to headlining rock clubs. The music press hailed him as a "fiddling sensation." He toured with Melissa Etheridge. He continued to hone his rock persona even as he released his second album, *Fine® Thank You Very Much,* a collection of traditional tunes with MacIsaac on fiddle and piano, and John Allan Cameron as guest acoustic guitarist.

Asked what he might do next, MacIsaac says anything is possible. "I can imagine watching *I Love Lucy* and instantly wanting to record a Cuban song," he says. "I'm not particularly limiting myself. I'd love to do Elvis onstage, except that I have a fiddle in my hands and can't move my arms."

Office of the Premier

QUEEN'S PARK

Many people dream of writing a hit song, and Bob Rae was no exception. He was premier of Ontario, leader of a New Democratic majority government. He occupied quarters on the second floor of the massive sandstone legislative buildings overlooking Queen's Park in the middle of downtown. Yet he hankered for something more.

On Christmas Eve 1993, midway through his single term of office, he wrote to Sony Music Canada seeking a wider audience for a song he had composed. "We're in the Same Boat Now," it is called, a tune about social harmony submitted on stationery emblazoned with his official seal.

"Some folks come here yesterday," the song begins colloquially, "some folks come from far away. Whether yesterday or far away, we're in the same boat now."

Back came the rejection slip.

"Though it is a fine piece of songwriting, it is not appropriate to what we are developing at this time in our domestic publishing division," company executive Michael Roth replied in the New Year. "Again, thank you for considering Sony Music and best of luck with your musical career."

Rae took the setback in stride. Within a day of receiving the notice, he went on MuchMusic to sing the ditty to his own piano accompaniment.

20 Sam the Record Man

347 YONGE STREET

Yes, this is Sam the Record Man. Several signs outside say so. The name "Sam" is also twice spelled from the rooftop in red block letters, and for good measure, giant images of two long-playing records and three compact discs adorn the building, each lit by sequential flashes of white neon so as to appear to spin.

Sam's is the most famous record store in the country, and probably the best-loved. It is the flagship of more than 200 Sam the Record Man outlets now operating coast to coast, and just as the number of outlets has proliferated over the years, so too has the square footage of the original store at Yonge and Gould Streets, one block north of the Eaton Centre. Incrementally, the store has encroached sideways and upwards through neighboring buildings, to create a ragged patchwork of rooms with scuffed grey floor tiles and bare fluorescent lighting.

Sam is Sam Sniderman. Among people who have never played an instrument or given up their day job, he ranks as one of the most important figures in Canadian music. In the early 1960s, he promoted Canadian artists to help establish a domestic recording industry, and through his nationwide expansion, he became a distributor of independent records for musicians who might otherwise never be heard outside their region.

"Do some good and make a profit – that's my philosophy," he says.

Sam discovered records when he was 17, in 1937. He was working for his older brother, Sid, installing car radios and performing other odd jobs at Sniderman Radio Sales and Service, at 714 College Street (in what is now Little Italy between Montrose Avenue and Crawford Street). The sales included RCA Victor products, and Sam would sometimes go to their nearby warehouse to pick up fresh inventory.

One day he bought a record player for himself, and two sets of 78-rpm recordings of Beethoven and Tchaikovsky. He enjoyed listening to them. He tried to talk Sid into letting him run a small record section in the store, but Sid said no. Radios were the hot item then; the record business was going downhill. Sam persisted, however, and

(Photo courtesy of Sam Sniderman)

Looking young and eager, Sam Sniderman stands amid the small record department he created in his brother's radio store at 714 College Street in the late 1930s. "Do some good and make and profit — that's my philosophy," he says.

eventually their mother intervened to let Sam open a record section that he kept expanding until, in 1951, the brothers renamed the store Sniderman's Music Hall.

After that, competition came mainly from A&A Records on Yonge Street – a scrappy rival, Sam recalls. "A&A would take our ads out of the newspapers, clip our name off the top, and plaster them in their own windows to match our discounts," he says. "Finally, I had our name run diagonally through the ads, thinking they couldn't use them, but they just cut the name out and put them back together. That did it for me. I spent hours sitting in a car outside A&A to see what kind of business they were doing. You can't really tell by sitting in a car, but I knew we had to be on Yonge Street."

In 1959, at Sam's urging, the brothers moved to a basement store on Yonge Street south of Dundas Street. Their sales doubled the first year. Later, a storefront became available north of Dundas. It looked ideal. It was the type of building the brothers were looking for, at a price they could afford. But Sam hesitated. Only the narrow Steele's Tavern stood between the available store and A&A Records.

"I was scared as all hell," he says. "I went to my mother, may she rest in peace, and I said, 'Ma, what'll I do? It's right next to the major competition.' And she said, 'Eaton's doesn't worry about Simpsons, so why are you worried about them?'"

On Labour Day, September 4, 1961, the new store opened as Sam the Record Man, becoming an instant landmark on the increasingly active Yonge Street strip. From the beginning, musicians and record-buyers alike mingled in the bargain-basement atmosphere, and Sam quickly became a fixture at the end of the checkout counter, smoking a big cigar. Sid was equally involved in running the store, but Sam acquired the public profile. More than a businessman, he became a father figure, benefactor, and confidant to an entire generation of musicians on the rise in the 1960s.

He has hundreds of stories.

"A young man came up to me one day on Yonge Street with a sign saying, 'I'm a Jewish boy, I'm willing to sell my blood to get a meal,'" he recalls. "It was Zal Yanovsky before he made it famous with the Lovin' Spoonful."

At the Mariposa Folk Festival one year, he remembers sitting on a bench when a young woman came up to him with her guitar.

"She said, 'Can I read you one of my poems?'

"I said, 'Sure.'

"She said, 'I'm just now setting this to music and I'd like your opinion.' The song was 'Both Sides Now,' and the woman was Joni Mitchell."

Whatever was happening in Canadian music, Sam seemed to be involved. When folk singer Gordon Lightfoot needed a room for his first news conference in the early 1960s, Sam and a friend put up $25 to rent space at the Steele's Tavern. When Canadian musicians began to push for more radio airplay in the late 1960s, Sam threw his support behind them to help bring about Canadian-content regulations. And when Sam himself began to open outlets across the country, he became the first national distributor for independent artists, his stores supporting an indie exchange that contributes, he says,

(Photo: Kathryn Exner)

Yes, this is Sam the Record Man. Several signs outside say so, and the name "Sam" is also twice spelled from the rooftop in red block letters.

"more to national unity than the House of Commons."

About the only person Sam ever failed to endear himself to was Mackenzie Kenner, owner of A&A Records. For years the two retailers waged a discount rivalry of rare proportions, outslashing each other's prices with special clearances, loss-leaders, and door-openers that turned Yonge north of Dundas into the city's top record-buying destination.

"We're friendly competitors," Sam told the *Globe and Mail* in 1967, "except that we'll stab each other in the back whenever we get the chance."

He wasn't joking.

Kenner, Sam says, "kept spitting on the sidewalk every time I'd go by. I wanted to be friendly with the guy – he's dead now – but he wouldn't have any part of me. I talked to my ma again. I said, 'Ma, what'll I do?' She said, 'If he doesn't want to talk to you, don't talk to him.'"

By 1970, the record store had become an established hangout, giving Sam the idea to open a nighttime gathering spot. He opened Sam the Chinese Food Man a few doors north of the store at 369 Yonge Street, above what was then Sam the Tape Man.

"The idea worked," he says. "All the artists came. I'll never forget Anne Murray, the first time she was singing at the Royal York Hotel. We had a bunch of kids, for some reason, who were coming up for lunch, and I called Anne to ask if she would show up and just see them. She's a good friend. She came to the restaurant, and graciously signed all the chopsticks. And I'll never forget – she showed up in a raincoat. She had probably gotten out of bed after being up late performing, and I swear to this day she had nothing on underneath."

Eventually the late hours became too much, and after 10 years, Sam ended his foray into the restaurant business. Another 10 years or so after that, A&A Records disappeared into bankruptcy. Not a trace of its past glory remains. The upstarts on the strip now are the British-owned HMV, a few doors south of Sam's, and American-owned Tower Records, at Yonge and Queen Streets. Their names never pass Sam's lips.

"When I see people who have a blue bag [from HMV]," he says, ever the arch competitor, "I ask them, 'Don't you like good music?'"

21

The Hard Rock Café (The Friar's Tavern)

283 YONGE STREET

An event that *Time* magazine once called "the most decisive moment in rock history" took place in what is now the Hard Rock Café.

The café occupies the north end of a building once called the Friar's Tavern, on Yonge Street opposite the Eaton Centre, one block south of Dundas Street. From 1964 to 1976, the Friar's served as one of the most popular nightclubs in the downtown core, and it was at the Friar's that Bob Dylan first met Levon and the Hawks, later renamed the Band. Today, anybody sitting at the Hard Rock's central bar, midway along the north wall, would be perched roughly where Levon Helm first settled down to his drum kit in the early morning of Thursday, September 16, 1965, to begin rehearsals for

(Photo: John Goddard)

The Hard Rock Café at 283 Yonge Street occupies the north end of what used to be the Friar's Tavern, where Bob Dylan first met Levon and the Hawks, later renamed the Band. The building opened in 1918 as a Childs Restaurant, part of a New York chain, featuring numerous windows and a bold, white terracotta face.

Dylan's stunning electric-debut tour that set the entire popular-music world on its ear.

"We rehearsed with Bob after they had locked up the place for the night," Helm recalls in his 1993 autobiography, *This Wheel's on Fire.* "The atmosphere was real friendly and exciting."

For the next decade, the careers of Bob Dylan and the Band were to remain closely associated, making their initial contact at the Friar's seem, in retrospect, almost inevitable. From September 1965 to the following May, they toured the United States, Canada, Australia, and northern Europe. Afterwards they settled together in Woodstock, New York. They made *The Basement Tapes,* toured widely again in 1974, released *Planet Waves* and a live album from the tour, then reunited in 1976 for the Band's farewell concert and film, *The Last Waltz.*

Mere weeks before their first encounter, however, any collaboration appeared unlikely. While Dylan had become the talk of America, the Hawks had barely heard of him. In their ignorance, they did not even like him. They viewed him as a folkie – a "strummer" they called him – and viewed themselves far more favorably as a dynamic, hard-edged bar band.

Levon and the Hawks claimed a colorful, evolutionary history. They took the name "Hawks" from their former front man, Ronnie Hawkins, a gregarious, hard-living rockabilly singer from Arkansas who first came to Canada in 1958. An agent had lured him and an earlier version of the Hawks first to nearby Hamilton, then to Toronto's Yonge Street. Hawkins loved Yonge Street. He called it "the Promised Land," where he brought a fading musical form to a brand-new audience.

With his greasy good looks and party attitude, Hawkins got Toronto hopping. He never learned to play an instrument, or to sing especially well, but he had his pick of gifted young musicians drawn to him for his showmanship and electrifying live performances. He tumbled. He did splits. He regularly launched himself into a double back flip off the stage, earning the nickname "Rompin' Ronnie."

"This band," guitarist Robbie Robertson once said of the original Hawks, "played the fastest, most violent rock and roll that I've ever heard."

One by one, all the Hawks who had come north from Arkansas returned south, except drummer Levon Helm. To fill the ranks, Hawkins hired locally, and by late 1961 the new lineup had stabilized at Helm (drums), Robertson (lead guitar), Rick Danko (bass), Garth Hudson (organ), and Richard Manuel (piano).

Hawkins rehearsed the young players endlessly. With his keen ear and staunch discipline, he

Rockabilly star Rompin' Ronnie Hawkins sashays through one of his earliest Toronto performances in March 1959, freshly arrived from Arkansas. He liked to call Yonge Street "the Promised Land."

(Photo courtesy of Ronnie Hawkins)

channelled their raw talent into a sound that was at once tight, controlled, and raging. After two years, however, relations between band leader and band grew strained. Hawkins would dock the pay of any member he caught smoking marijuana or bringing a girlfriend to a show. He preferred drinkers to potheads, he said, and he insisted that his players appear sexually available, in order to attract women to the shows, who would attract men. More problematic, Hawkins remained musically conservative. "Anything more than three chords is progressive jazz to me," he once said, only half-jokingly. He insisted on sticking to a proven formula, as the others began to move from rockabilly to rhythm-and-blues.

For his entire career, Hawkins has faced the same recurring problem: he develops musicians only to have them grow beyond him. His distinguished alumni also include pianist and composer David Foster, Hamilton blues singer King Biscuit Boy, the members of Crowbar (best known for their 1971 hit "Oh What a Feeling"), and most of the members of the Full Tilt Boogie Band, the last group to back Janis Joplin. Levon and the Hawks left him in late 1963. By the new year, they were booking dates on their own, first at the Friar's, then at other clubs already familiar to them, such as the nearby Le Coq d'Or.

One of their biggest fans in those early days was Mary Martin, the main person who would later lead them to Dylan. She works now as a talent scout in Nashville, but was born and raised in Toronto. "I went to Havergal," she says, referring to the private girls' school at Avenue Road and Lawrence Avenue, "and I went to the University of British Columbia, briefly, and when I came back in disgrace I was told that I had had my chance at university, so I'd better go and get a job."

She found work first at the Crown Life Insurance Company, but left soon afterwards to live with friends in New York's Greenwich

Village. The year was 1963. By chance she landed a receptionist's job with Albert Grossman, manager at the time to the hottest acts in folk music – Peter, Paul and Mary; Ian and Sylvia; and Bob Dylan. "Then I was told that I would go nowhere in the music industry if I didn't know how to be a secretary," Martin recalls. "I believed that, and every so often I would go back to Toronto for a couple of months to learn shorthand and typing and stuff like that."

In Toronto, Martin hung out mostly with a woman named Toni Trow, now Toni Myers, a filmmaker in Toronto and still a good friend. "We would go to drink at the Pilot Tavern near Yonge and Bloor," Martin says. "Then after several beers, or gin-and-tonics, we'd go down to see the Hawks at 'the Le Coq d'Or,' as everybody called it, and basically just be groupies and musical fans."

The Hawks, after leaving Hawkins, retained their tight, intense sound, while also becoming more versatile. They played early rock-and-roll numbers such as Barrett Strong's "Money" and Chuck Berry's "No Particular Place to Go." They sang slow, soulful ballads such as "Georgia on My Mind." They invented their own arrangements of hot rhythm-and-blues numbers such as the Isley Brothers' "Shout" and James Brown's "Please Please Please." Helm figured as nominal leader and torchbearer of the group's southern roots, but otherwise the members dispensed with an obvious front man. They preferred to rotate lead vocals and sometimes instruments, a practice that later became their trademark as the Band.

"Those boys talked to each other musically," Martin says. "They had conversations with themselves that were so deeply musical that if you listened, you got to go along. They were the best band that we had ever, ever heard, and they took you to dreamland."

Another early fan, also with a Dylan connection, was John Hammond Jr., son of the legendary music executive who had signed Dylan to Columbia, and a solo blues artist in his own right who had hung out with Dylan in Greenwich Village. In early 1964, while in Toronto to play at the Purple Onion, Hammond went to hear the Hawks. "They were a *really* hot R&B band," he recalls in *Across the Great Divide: The Band and America,* by Barney Hoskyns. "Each of them had their own little showcase spots, doing Junior Parker and T-Bone Walker covers, and Robbie was the most intense, heavy-duty electric guitar player I have ever heard."

Helm says that the Hawks considered themselves "the undisputed champions of Canadian rock and roll." But they were still playing bars. In search of something bigger, they started travelling to New York every chance they got, cutting an unsuccessful single there in early 1964, and in June of that year landing a two-week engagement at the Peppermint Lounge in Manhattan, famous for the Peppermint Twist.

When Hammond heard that the Hawks were in town, he invited them to play on his third album, *So Many Roads.* "He was one of the first to see the possibilities of having an electric band," Helm says. The Hawks jumped at the chance, although in the end only Robertson, Helm, and Hudson played on the record, along with three musicians the record company had already hired – Charlie Musselwhite on harmonica, Jimmy Lewis on bass, and Chicago blues guitarist Michael Bloomfield, who played piano in deference to Robertson's superior prowess on guitar.

The following year, in early 1965, the Hawks were still looking for their own record deal. They returned to New York to cut another single that proved unsuccessful, and a couple of months later in Toronto, made a demo tape to send to various New York companies. Mary Martin heard the demo tracks and remembers them as "shuck-and-jive bluesy things," meaning derivative and unexceptional. "They never flew," she says.

By then, Martin was back full time with Albert Grossman. Through Toni Trow, she also continued to follow the Hawks, putting herself in position to become a matchmaker. Martin passed a copy of the demo tape to Grossman's assistant, John Court, hoping to interest him. "He was a really neat guy," she says, "but he was a jazzer and he said, 'Miss Martin, we aren't interested in talent of that calibre' – meaning, I suppose, 'They're a bar band. Who cares?'"

At the same time, she noticed that Dylan was becoming agitated. She dates the period to April 1965, when a new group called the Byrds recorded an electric version of Dylan's "Mr. Tambourine Man."

"He was just sitting in the office sort of shaking his leg and his head, going, 'Golly, what do I do next, huh?'" Martin recalls. "And what had happened is very simple to explain. Bob Dylan had heard drums, an electric bass, and an electric guitar on 'Mr. Tambourine Man' – and for a folk singer that was a giant leap to think, 'Damn, now I'm going to have to get a band.' But that's really what he had to ponder. And he did ponder it, and I said, 'Well, go to Toronto and see the Hawks.'"

Dylan did not go right away. He went to England, and Dylan's biographers all agree that he went through some kind of profound dissatisfaction that spring. Being a folk hero now bored him, he said. He was fed up with playing guitar and harmonica alone in front of reverential sold-out crowds. D.A. Pennebaker's film *Don't Look Back,* shot between late April and mid-May during a concert tour of England, closely documents Dylan's addled state of mind. At one point before walking onstage, he says, "I don't feel like singing."

Dylan returned from England in early June. Soon afterwards he wrote "Like a Rolling Stone," and on the 15th he recorded it in New York, a six-minute masterpiece that represented, in the words of biographer Paul Williams, "a whole new kind of music." It wasn't folk. It wasn't rock and roll. It was something else – a rich, stately release, perhaps, of all the restlessness and boredom that Dylan had been feeling that spring.

With him in the studio was an electric band consisting of three experienced session players, a novice organist named Al Kooper, and guitarist Michael Bloomfield, who had played on *So Many Roads*. The following day, the group recorded three or four more songs towards what would become Dylan's sixth album, *Highway 61 Revisited*. On July 20, "Like a Rolling Stone" was released as a single, and five days after that, at the Newport Folk Festival, Dylan made his first stage appearance with an electric band.

He was scheduled as a solo performer, but had arrived the night before to recruit five players from other acts, including Kooper and Bloomfield. Onstage with them, he roared through "Maggie's Farm," "Like a Rolling Stone," and "It Takes a Lot to Laugh, It Takes a Train to Cry." People in the crowd booed. One theory has it that they were actually booing the sound mix – that they couldn't hear Dylan's voice – but Martin, who was there, says no. "It was a reaction in point-blank terms to amplification," she says. When the band left the stage, organizers appealed to Dylan to go back and perform solo. He returned to sing "It's All Over Now, Baby Blue" – giving the title an ironic meaning – and an acoustic version of "Mr. Tambourine Man."

Watching Dylan that night stiffened Martin's resolve to play go-between. "Bob Dylan still needed his own band," she says, "and I really felt that the boys needed to take that other step before they really emerged."

The Hawks were playing all summer at Tony Mart's Nite Spot, a huge teenage club in Somers Point, New Jersey, south of Atlantic City. Martin persuaded a Grossman scout, Danny Weiner, to check them out. She also told the Hawks about Dylan's explosive Newport concert, and in early August she took Rick Danko an advance copy of *Highway 61 Revisited*. A week or so later, Helm received a phone call backstage.

"This is Bob Dylan calling," the voice on the other end said, as Helm remembers the conversation.

"Yes, sir," Helm replied. "What can I do for you?"

"Well, um … uh, how'dya like to play the Hollywood Bowl?"

A pause. "Who else is on the bill?"

"Just us," Dylan said.

Helm told Dylan he would think about it and call back the next day. He and the other band members "had no idea how big Bob Dylan was," Helm says in his book. They were still calling him a strummer and mispronouncing his name as "Bob Dielan."

"The root of the band was Levon, and the root of Levon was R&B," Martin says to explain the Hawks' attitude. "Folk music was diametrically opposite." But their resistance still seems astounding, given the phenomenon Dylan had become.

One year earlier, Bob Dylan had been a success. By August 1965, he was a sensation. At 24 years old, he stood at the centre of a new music that critics were calling folk-rock and that Dylan himself refused to label. Sound, lyrics, and emotion swirled and fit together in his songs in revolutionary new ways. "The geometry of innocent flesh on the bone causes Galileo's math book to get thrown," he sang in "Tombstone Blues." "Ezra Pound and T.S. Eliot are fighting in the captain's tower, while calypso singers laugh at them and fishermen hold flowers," he sang in "Desolation Row."

All that August, "Like a Rolling Stone" rode near the top of the charts, soon to be followed by "Positively Fourth Street." Other artists scrambled to record Dylan songs and sing in the Dylan style. Cher scored a hit with "All I Really Want to Do." The Turtles did the same with "It Ain't Me Babe." That month alone, 48 Dylan songs were released by other people, and Barry McGuire was on his way to a number 1 hit with a blatant ripoff, "Eve of Destruction."

"There's a new swinging mood in the country," said Murray the K, the New York disc jockey, "and Bobby baby is definitely what's happening, baby."

But if the Hawks were not entirely sold on Dylan, neither was Dylan sold on the Hawks. His first choice on guitar was Mike Bloomfield. Only after Bloomfield turned him down to meet other commitments did Dylan turn to Robbie Robertson. He knew of Robertson through Bloomfield, Hammond, and Mary Martin, but usually credits Martin for the connection. "Mary was a rather per-severing soul," he once told *Rolling Stone* editor Jann Wenner. "She knew all the bands and singers from Canada, and she kept pushing these guys the Hawks on me."

Dylan invited Robertson to New York. He asked Robertson's advice on buying an electric guitar and took him to rehearse infor-mally with other musicians Dylan was scouting. Robertson suggested replacing the drummer with Levon Helm, at which point Dylan invited Helm to join, but at first there was no long-term deal. The other Hawks would continue to play at Tony Mart's, while Robertson and Helm played two electric concerts with Dylan.

The first took place on August 28, 1965, at the Forest Hills Tennis Stadium in Queens, New York City. The audience was the biggest Robertson and Helm had ever performed for – 15,000 people. Dylan divided the concert into two sets. In the first, he sang seven numbers by himself with an acoustic guitar and harmonica. An intermission followed. Then came the electric set, with Al Kooper on organ, Harvey Brooks on bass, Robertson on lead guitar, and Helm on drums. Before they went on, Helm says, Dylan gathered them together and said, "Just keep playing, no matter how weird it gets."

Boos and catcalls followed. "Yeah, yeah, shake it up, baby." "Scumbag." "Where's Ringo?" A fight broke out. People threw fruit at the band members, although not at Dylan, and at one point a

young man rushed the stage and
knocked Kooper off his chair. The
scene, says Helm, "was looking
ugly." After Newport, booing must
have seemed like the thing to do,
but a whole generation of students
who had looked to Dylan as a
plain-speaking folk hero was also
having a genuine problem adjust-
ing. The second set went 90
minutes and Albert Grossman,
fearing trouble, ordered an end
without an encore. Six days
later, the group repeated the
show to a more receptive crowd
at the Hollywood Bowl.

Bob Dylan takes the stage at Maple Leaf
Gardens on October 12, 1978, his electric
guitar by then taken for granted. "Bobby
baby is definitely what's happening, baby,"
disc jockey Murray the K said when Dylan's
sound was sweeping the music world in the
mid-1960s.

(Photo: Tom Robe)

The concerts left Dylan
ecstatic. "Let 'em boo all they
want," Helm recalls him saying. "Sells tickets." Dylan proposed to take the band on tour,
but Kooper said he'd had enough – the booing had put him off.

Helm said he would not break up the Hawks. "Take us all, or
don't take anybody," he told Grossman, and Dylan replied, "When
can I hear the band?"

On Wednesday afternoon, September 15, 1965, Dylan arrived in
Toronto. At midnight, he went to the Friar's Tavern to watch Levon
and the Hawks play their final set, and he rehearsed with them
afterwards until 6 a.m.

He rehearsed with the Hawks all Thursday night as well, and at
one point he gave an interview to the renowned cultural commentator

Robert Fulford, then a reporter for the *Toronto Star*. Fulford asked Dylan if his current work was being influenced by anybody, the way his early work had been influenced by Woody Guthrie.

"It's all sort of formed in its own way now," Dylan replied. "It's not influenced by anyone. I know my thing now, I know what it is. It's hard to describe. I don't know what to call it because I've never heard it before."

22 Church of the Holy Trinity

19 TRINITY SQUARE

"If you walk through the church clapping your hands, you will hear it," says Peter Moore, an independent record producer with especially keen ears. "In about the rear third there's a 'sweet spot,' I call it. You clap your hands and this amazing, beautiful decay takes place."

He is talking about the Church of the Holy Trinity. It stands now in the shadow of the latter-day cathedral to consumerism, the Eaton Centre, but when the church opened in 1847, it presided over what was then the working-class neighborhood of Macaulaytown. Some churches stand on street corners and announce themselves with spires; the Holy Trinity rose Gothic-style to command the entire district by virtue of disproportionately high walls.

The height partly accounts for the amazing reverb decay that Moore and other producers love. For years, CBC Radio used Holy

Trinity for live Thursday broadcasts of *Music Around Us,* and the congregation now sponsors Monday noon-hour concerts from May to October. Classical musicians have recorded there, as have choral groups and baroque and medieval ensembles. In late 1987, Moore rented the building for a single 14-hour stretch to record *The Trinity Session* – the bewitching album that launched the Cowboy Junkies.

"A remarkable live set," *Rolling Stone* magazine said in a four-star review. "The best and most authentic version I have ever heard," Lou Reed said of the group's rendition of his song "Sweet Jane." Almost overnight, the Cowboy Junkies went from playing Queen Street West to touring North America, Europe, and Japan.

(Photo: John Goddard)

Once the centrepiece of the working-class neighborhood of Macaulaytown, the Church of the Holy Trinity stands now in the shadow of a latter-day cathedral to consumerism, the Eaton Centre. The Cowboy Junkies rented the church on November 27, 1987, to record their surprise breakthrough album, *The Trinity Session.*

"It's amazing the effect that album has on people," Moore says now. "I remember getting letters saying, 'I'm just getting off my cocaine addiction and I don't think I could have done it without *The Trinity Session*' – stuff like that."

Moore is an aural guerrilla. He is known for his ability to work cheaply outside a studio in spaces that he finds acoustically beguiling. One day he might be recording a 30-piece orchestra for a television soundtrack at Holy Trinity; the next he might be taping a rock band for an independent label at the

RPM Club (now the Guvernment), at the foot of Jarvis Street.

He got his start in 1976, he says, at the University of Western Ontario. He enrolled as an anthropology student and spent his spare time helping to establish a campus radio station, CHRW. Soon he had his own punk and new-wave show, featuring the raw new music coming out of New York, Toronto, and London, England.

"The problem was that there was no way on earth that I could meet Canadian-content rules," he says. "Nobody was recording the Canadian punk bands, so I just started going out myself, recording the ones playing around town. I basically just bootlegged them. They were happy because they got airplay, and I was happy because I kept my show."

On a student budget, Moore found himself limited in the way that record producers in the 1930s and 1940s were limited. He possessed no headphones, no multitracks, no punch-in capability, only a single microphone at which to arrange instruments and vocals for a series of live takes. The constraint led him to experiment with what he calls a "minimalist miking technique."

"I remember I picked up a Billie Holiday record made in 1956, the year I was born," he says. "It was a simple one-mike recording, and I thought, 'Wow, nothing wrong with this.' So I started on a quest of finding out as much as I could about the old-fashioned way of recording with one mike. Technology drives us forward, but sometimes we forget that there are a lot of good things about the old ways. I started working out a methodology. You know, 'Where do I put the drums? Where do I put the bass? Where do I put the different band members in front of the microphone?'"

By the mid-1980s, better established as an independent producer, Moore was using what he calls a four-capsule ambisonic microphone – "developed by the British navy to spot Soviet submarines." It registered sound from all directions, including top and bottom, an

(Photo: Noel Archambault)

Musicians for *The Trinity Session* encircle Peter Moore's four-capsule, ambisonic microphone during sound checks at the "sweet spot" inside the Church of the Holy Trinity. "I choreographed everything," Moore says.

advance that allowed him to arrange musicians completely around a microphone instead of only in front.

At about the same time he met the Cowboy Junkies. They were a laid-back, bluesy, country-influenced group consisting of two brothers, a sister, and a childhood friend: Michael Timmins (guitar), Peter Timmins (drums), Margo Timmins (vocals), and Alan Anton (bass). They told him they wanted to cut a record in their rehearsal garage but didn't know how.

Moore said he would show them. In October 1986, he took his four-capsule microphone to the garage and recorded *Whites Off Earth Now!,* the band's first independent CD. It sold 3,000 copies, a success by the band's standards at the time. Afterwards, the Junkies suggested they record another album at a different location. Moore recommended the church.

"Recorded live at the Church of the Holy Trinity in Toronto, Canada, on November 27, 1987," the liner notes read. The day began at around 9 a.m., with Moore clearing the pews from the back third of the nave and setting his microphone at the "sweet spot." Five extra players showed up. They brought fiddles, mandolins, harmonicas, a Dobro hillbilly-style guitar, and a pedal steel guitar. Moore spent most of the day arranging everybody in a circle and experimenting with positions around the microphone.

"I choreographed everything," he says. "I marked the spot where the mandolin player would stand, and when his solo came up, he would actually walk up to the mike, do his solo, and move back again."

By about 5 p.m., he was ready to tape. By 11:30 p.m., the church janitor was helping everybody out the door. In 14 hours, the group had completed all 12 tracks at a cost of $125 for the church rental, plus the price of a party-size pizza.

"I remember it all coming together," says Michael Timmins, the band's lead guitarist and guiding force. "The first half [of the day] was very stressful because it took a long time to get the proper places and to find the right sound. That took six or seven hours, and it was tense because we knew we had to be out of there by a certain time. But once the music started happening, it was amazing. It was like the sun coming out from behind a cloud or something. Everything started to gel, to happen really beautifully, and without any effort really. I remember hearing all the instruments that we hadn't really worked with before, hearing them echoing through the church, and just feeling great about it. We all knew we were playing well and creating something really

(Photo: Noel Archambault)

Tedium shows on the face of Cowboy Junkies lead vocalist Margo Timmins during the recording of *The Trinity Session*. "It took a long time to find the right sound," says her brother Michael.

special. We didn't know if anybody else would recognize that or not, but for us it was a brilliant day."

"That recording," says Moore, "was so well received because of the sound – the sound of the church, the choice of songs, Margo's delicate delivery on vocals, the playing by everybody. Technically, the reverb decay is such that it makes a player play in a different way, but spiritually, too, just the whole idea of being in a beautiful church creates a whole kind of vibe."

The band released the record independently at first, saying they would regard sales of 5,000 copies as "really successful." Six months later, RCA picked it up and sold a million copies worldwide.

23

St. Michael's Choir School

66 BOND STREET

For seven giddy weeks in the summer of 1954, the number 1 record on the continent was "Sh-Boom" by the Crew-Cuts. The lyrics began:

Hey nonny ding dong, a lang a lang a lang,

Boom vah doe, ba-do ba-do ba-vayk.

Two months later, the quartet followed with "Oop Shoop," said to be "Sh-Boom" spelled sideways. All four vocalists were products of St. Michael's Choir School, trained from early boyhood to sing Latin motets in vaulted cathedrals, but preferring on graduation to perform doo-wop versions of black rhythm-and-blues hits in American nightclubs. "Not all the boys can find their vocation in church music," Monsignor Edward Ronan, the school's founder, observed dryly at the time.

Ronan began the choir program in 1937 in a single room of an office building at 67 Bond Street, next to St. Michael's Cathedral,

Monsignor Edward Ronan, founder of the St. Michael's Choir School, conducts a choral group featuring four of the school's most famous graduates, the Four Lads, during a television show in the late 1950s.

the seat of the Roman Catholic archdiocese of Toronto. Through a mix of musical and academic classes at the elementary level, he aspired to develop singers, organists, and choirmasters for local parishes. Slowly the program expanded. In 1942, Ronan added Grades 9 and 10. In 1950, he moved the entire program into its own building across the street at number 66, a red-brick schoolhouse embellished with Gothic spires and arches. Now the program occupies parts of three buildings at 66, 67, and 69 Bond Street, offering classes to as many as 360 boys from Grade 3 to the end of high school.

Pop fame first struck the program in 1949. Four graduates calling themselves the Four Lads went on Elwood Glover's *Canadian Cavalcade,* on CBC Radio. The quartet's members were Jimmie Arnold (lead tenor), Bernie Toorish (tenor and arranger), Frankie Busseri (baritone), and Connie Codarini (bass). Afterwards they left for New York, appearing for more than six months at Le Ruban Bleu nightclub, then working as studio vocalists at Columbia Records. They backed popular American crooner Johnnie Ray on such hits as "Cry" and "Little White Cloud," and sang on Frankie Laine's

"Rain, Rain, Rain." They also cut records of their own. In their 10 years together they made several albums and about 20 singles, including "Istanbul" (1953) and their million-sellers "Moments to Remember" (1955) and "No, Not Much" (1956).

The Crew-Cuts trailed the Four Lads by about three years. They consisted of Pat Barrett (lead tenor), John Perkins (second tenor), John's younger brother Ray (bass), and Rudi Maugeri (baritone and arranger). Originally formed as the Four Tones in 1952, they changed their name first to the Canadaires and then to the Crew-Cuts after barbering their hair identically to define their image, nine years before the Beatles.

"When we all get older, we'll change the name to the Skinheads," their manager, Fred Strauss, said at a time when being a skinhead simply meant being bald.

"Sh-Boom" turned out to be the group's greatest hit. "Oop Shoop" and "Crazy 'Bout You Baby" also sold well in 1954, and they scored again the following year with "Earth Angel" and "Don't Be Angry" – part of a 10-year recording career that included nine albums. Both the Crew-Cuts and the Four Lads received lifetime achievement awards at the 1984 Juno ceremonies, along with the Diamonds, another group formed in the same era at the University of Toronto.

"We have always been proud of them," Monsignor Barrett Armstrong, the current director, says of the choir school's distin-guished alumni. Pop fame has not touched the school lately, but six CDs of the choirboys singing with orchestra are for sale at the school and cathedral.

24

Massey Hall

178 VICTORIA STREET

Massey Hall opened in 1894 as the first building in the country designed expressly for concerts. Classical-music lovers esteem it as the original home of the Toronto Symphony Orchestra and the Toronto Mendelssohn Choir. Jazz lovers prize it as the site of the great 1953 concert in which Charlie Parker, Dizzy Gillespie, Charles Mingus, Max Roach, and Bud Powell recorded together live. Folk listeners associate it particularly with Gordon Lightfoot, whose single concert there in 1967 became the first of an annual series until 1984; it now continues every 18 months. Rock audiences know it for concerts by Rush, Cream, George Thorogood, and Keith Richards. For blues fans, too, Massey Hall holds special significance: here, on February 23, 1970, Lonnie Johnson, the father of the modern blues guitar, performed publicly for the last time.

(Photo: Jim McHarg)

"Everybody just loved Lonnie," says jazz-band leader Jim McHarg of Lonnie Johnson, shown here in Toronto in 1965. Recognized as the father of the modern blues guitar, Johnson made an emotional final appearance five years later at Massey Hall.

Johnson lived his last five years in Toronto. He arrived to play a two-week engagement in late June 1965 and stayed until his death, on June 16, 1970. Of his earliest beginnings, little is known: his year of birth has been given variously as 1889, 1894, 1899, and 1900. What is certain is that he was born into a musical family in New Orleans and began playing violin in his father's string band at age 14. In 1917, he joined a musical revue in England, and two years later, returned home to discover that Spanish influenza had killed his parents and all of his 10 or 12 siblings except a brother, James "Steady Roll" Johnson, a piano player. The brothers moved to St. Louis to play with jazz bands on Mississippi steamboats, after which Lonnie began to travel widely, spending long periods in Texas, New York, and Chicago.

Lonnie Johnson is recognized now as the first great modern blues guitarist. His influence has been enormous. He is credited with having originated the blues guitar solo, picking note by note with accents, elongations, and arpeggios, and he was the first to use the guitar as a "crying" counterpoint to lyrics, an idea since elaborated on by everybody from T-Bone Walker to B.B. King to Jimmy Page. Robert (Leroy) Spencer, now revered as "King of the Delta Blues Singers," changed his name to Robert (Lonnie) Johnson in the man's honor.

Lonnie Johnson never became rich, but neither did he see himself as a down-and-dirty blues man. He played a clean, manicured guitar style with a delightful sense of swing and sophistication. His songwriting and singing, too, were sophisticated and urbane, and he took pains to distance himself from the rougher country-blues styles of such people as Lightnin' Hopkins and John Lee Hooker – artists who eventually became more popular than himself. Johnson brought blues to jazz and jazz to blues, producing some 130 recordings between 1925 and 1932 with such greats as Louis Armstrong, Duke Ellington, and fellow guitarist Eddie Lang. Johnson's back-and-forth solos with Armstrong's trumpet on the 1927 recordings "I'm Not Rough," "Hotter Than That," and "Savoy Blues" remain special moments in early jazz history, as does his guitar work on the Ellington classic "The Mooche."

A jazz person brought Johnson to Toronto in 1965, and a blues person later booked him at Massey Hall. The jazz person is Jim McHarg, a double-bass player from Glasgow, Scotland, who, after performing with Britain's top jazz musicians in the 1950s, settled in Toronto as leader of a traditional jazz band called Jim McHarg's Metro Stompers. During the mid- to late 1960s, the Metro Stompers reigned as the city's most popular jazz group, playing at the Penny Farthing coffeehouse (at 110–112 Yorkville Avenue, now a clothing boutique) every Friday and Saturday night. The blues person is Richard Flohil, an Englishman who emigrated to Chicago in the 1950s mainly to meet Muddy Waters, and later moved to Toronto as a blues promoter. Both remember Johnson with deep affection; each vividly recalls his last hurrah.

———

JIM McHARG, *current leader of Jim McHarg's Jazzmen*
"Lonnie Johnson walked into one of the healthiest music environments in Canada ever – Yorkville in the mid-1960s. Folk music, traditional

jazz, pop, and rock all mingled together in the same place, with everybody respecting each other, and no rancor of any kind. We were all part of one big scene. The Metro Stompers were very, very successful there, and everybody just loved Lonnie. Everybody.

"John McHugh was the one who actually brought him to Toronto. John was the owner of the Penny Farthing, an English guy, a great traditional jazz fan, a lover of all kinds of music, and somebody with a great knowledge of all these people. I sold him on the idea of bringing Lonnie up for a couple of weeks to play on his own and alternately with my band.

"John and I went down to the bus terminal to meet him. We were a little nervous. Lonnie was arriving on the overnight bus from New York, and we started wondering if we had made a mistake bringing this old, old guy to Yorkville to compete with all the good-looking folk singers and blaring rock-and-roll bands. But Lonnie walked off the bus like a kid. He had the step of a 50-year-old. He was just so pleased to be here, and all he wanted to do was to play.

"His opening at the Penny Farthing that night was absolutely electrifying. He is without a doubt the greatest performer I have ever seen. He played his upbeat jazz numbers, his sweet ballads, his authentic blues songs, and the audience applauded everything he did. Within 24 hours the word was out, and Lonnie never left Toronto. He played at the Penny for months and months and months. He played other clubs. He played all kinds of gigs without a band, and we took him places with us when we could get him. I remember there was one club in the Village where the owner cheated absolutely every musician he ever met except Lonnie Johnson. Lonnie always got paid. There was something about Lonnie that people liked. He had a sort of charisma. You would walk down Yorkville Avenue with him, and 16-year-old kids would all know him and go out of their way to be kind to him.

"Lonnie Johnson was like a shrine. I look on Lonnie the way I look on Bessie Smith and Louis Armstrong and all the other great black singers and instrumentalists who really started blues and jazz. Lonnie was part of the history and the legend of the blues. He was an originator in his instrument, an absolutely authentic blues performer, a beautiful ballad singer, but also a pop-song writer with an ability to compose nice, ordinary songs that people liked. He was sort of a crossover artist who did everything he did very well. This didn't always sit so well with everybody. Some people might want to hear his instrumental side and he would be singing the softer songs, or some people might want the blues thing. But Lonnie was always his own man. He would actually go in front of a blues audience and sing what they might see as a trite, sugary ballad. He would do what he wanted to do and sing what he wanted to sing. He was a free spirit, and I think that's one of the reasons why Lonnie loved Toronto so much – because he was actually accepted as Lonnie Johnson. Not many people tried to force him into a pigeonhole.

"That November, somebody at Columbia Records thought it would be a great idea for the Metro Stompers to make a record with Lonnie, the kind of thing we were doing together at the Penny Farthing. They gave us three hours of studio time down on Mutual Street. The album is called *Stompin' at the Penny with Jim McHarg's Metro Stompers, featuring Lonnie Johnson.*

"On the album Lonnie sings one ballad, 'My Mother's Eyes,' one jazz number, 'Go Go Swing,' and two blues songs, 'Mr. Blues Walks' and 'Bring It on Home to Mama.' Most important to us, he also plays guitar on 'China Boy' and 'West End Blues,' just the way he played with Louis Armstrong and Duke Ellington. On 'China Boy,' he just soars. He's fantastic.

"There were only 1,000 records pressed. Now it's out on CD and playing on the radio, but at the time it was a very local thing. We were just pleased to record with Lonnie. To me, traditional jazz is black, and Lonnie was black, and for me to play with Lonnie was very, very rewarding for that reason. I'm not saying that what some of these white bands have done in Europe and other places is unimportant, because what we do is an art form in its own way. But to play authentic jazz, you have to be born black, you have to have been part of that environment, and I think subliminally what we were doing with Lonnie was saying, 'Thanks Lonnie, thanks Louis, thanks Ella Fitzgerald, thanks Ray Brown, thanks everybody, for giving us this wonderful music.'

"In 1969, Lonnie got hit by a taxi. It happened on Avenue Road right outside Webster's Restaurant [now Gabbeh Persian Rug Gallery, south of Davenport Road at Webster Street]. Lonnie was walking along, and a taxi jumped the curb and hit him. What was so unusual about this is that I was driving south on Avenue Road, and I saw the ambulance and a stretcher going into it. I actually drove past the accident. I was thinking, 'Oh, some poor guy got hit by a car,' and when I got home I got a call from a friend named Billy O'Connor and he said, 'Lonnie's in hospital. He's just been knocked down on Avenue Road.'

"After that we did a few things for Lonnie. We got some concerts going. We threw a benefit at the Ryerson Theatre with a number of people, including Ian and Sylvia. Gordon Lightfoot didn't do the benefit, but he donated $500, which was a lot of money back then. It was a major contribution. The Toronto Musicians Association gave a tremendous help. Even the insurance company was very helpful. Nobody was going to give Lonnie a hard time.

"A few months later, Dick Flohil, who puts on all the blues shows, said he'd like to get Lonnie down to Massey Hall to play with Buddy Guy and Bobby 'Blue' Bland. He came to me because people kind of looked to me as Lonnie's keeper. I could be quite vicious trying to protect the old guy, but I thought, 'This could be a great idea. I know Lonnie would want to do this.'

"The only trouble was, I knew that once Lonnie got started, he wouldn't want to stop. Even before the accident, John McHugh and I used to worry about his health. We would insist on a 30-minute set, and we devised a system where we would stand up in front of him to signal when it was time to come off. But it didn't work so well. Every time John or I stood up, Lonnie just closed his eyes and went right on singing. At one point we actually got an alarm clock, and the alarm would ring right in the middle of a song. It was quite funny, actually. We had to do this just to get him off, otherwise he would never have rested. So I told Dick Flohil that Lonnie could appear on condition that I go on with him to keep an eye on things and see that he wasn't going to kill himself. We would do only two numbers, and that would be it.

"I'll always be happy we did it, because the performance turned out to be Lonnie's last. Everything worked out beautifully. We got him off after two numbers, and what a send-off – hundreds of kids screaming for him. The audience was all young people, almost like a rock-and-roll audience, and Bobby Bland and Buddy Guy were obviously thrilled to have him onstage. They knew that Lonnie was one of the originals, one of the people who gave everybody else the concepts. There was an incredible bit of love there. It was a fabulous last appearance for Lonnie, thanks to Dick Flohil, who thought of getting him up there."

RICHARD FLOHIL, *promoter*
"That concert was one of the most moving things that I have ever, ever had the sheer privilege to get involved with. Twenty-five years later, people still come up to me and say, 'Oh, that was an amazing show.'

"I had arranged to bring in Bobby 'Blue' Bland, who I'm a major fan of, and Buddy Guy, and we called the show Blue Monday. It was on a Monday night. I also brought in a local band called Whiskey Howl, who opened the show. We sat Lonnie in the audience in the third or fourth row at the centre, with the idea of bringing him onstage.

"Lonnie had been in a traffic accident. He had gone into the hospital, and in the hospital he had had a stroke, so he was paralysed up one side. He couldn't play. We brought him up from the audience, he sat on a stool, and Buddy Guy played acoustic guitar for him. Buddy very rarely plays acoustic guitar, but I remember how well he duplicated the sort of style that Lonnie had. So it was Buddy playing guitar, Jim McHarg playing bass, and Lonnie just singing.

"While he was singing, many of the guys in Bobby's band, including Bobby, sort of filtered out onstage to watch. There are no wings in Massey Hall, so to hear Lonnie they walked out and stood at the back of the stage out of the spotlight. Lonnie sang two numbers. He got a standing ovation; the audience was just so touched. You could not fail to be touched by this frail old man sitting on a stool with one of the hottest guitarists in the world playing acoustic guitar very gently and quietly and sinuously behind him as he sang these two songs. And when Lonnie left the stage, tears were pouring down his face. It was a very, very emotional moment.

"Lonnie Johnson was certainly one of the most influential guitarists in the history of blues. He was certainly one of the most popular artists of the genre in the thirties and early forties, before it became electric. People like Bobby Bland and Buddy Guy and others, including B.B. King, were all very much in this man's debt. To this day, B.B. King will tell you that Lonnie Johnson was one of the people who influenced him most.

"About one year earlier, I had the privilege of introducing them. B.B. King came into town and he phoned me. He had arrived a day early and had the day free, which was about as rare in B.'s life as you can imagine. He was staying at the Lord Simcoe Hotel down on King Street, now defunct, in a room the size of a shoebox. He phoned me up and said, 'I've never ever met Lonnie Johnson. I hear he lives in Toronto. Do you know where he is?'

"I said, 'Well, no, but give me a second and I'll make a couple of calls.' So I called a guy named Howard Mathews. Howard at that time was one of the owners of the Underground Railroad, which was one of the first soul-food restaurants, and is the husband, incidentally, of Salome Bey. I knew he was also a friend of Lonnie's, so I called Howie and said, 'Have you any idea where Lonnie is?'

"He said, 'Well, sure. He's sitting in my living-room.'

"So I drove down from my suburban home in Willowdale and picked up B. in my rusty old Toyota, and we drove to Howard's house. He was living on a tiny little street called Maribeth in the Sherbourne–Carlton area, directly behind the old Diamond Club, now the Phoenix. I guess we arrived at 9 or 9:30 at night, something like that. We walked into the house, and there was not only Lonnie Johnson but Sonny Terry and Brownie McGhee as well. I just went, 'Whoa, this is great,' and they all got down to a lot of wonderful talk and conversation. And that's how B.B. King met Lonnie Johnson."

25

Nathan Phillips Square

CITY HALL, 100 QUEEN STREET WEST

Guidelines for the use of the plaza in front of City Hall prohibit events that might objectify men or women through sexual stereotyping. In that spirit, civic authorities refuse to allow beauty pageants to be held there, and once bluntly rejected a permit for a bikini contest. A few days before the city's 1991 New Year's Eve bash, officials also cancelled a performance by Barenaked Ladies.

"If your mother or my mother saw a headline saying, 'City of Toronto presents Barenaked Ladies,' they'd be really concerned," events co-ordinator Dawna Proudman said at the time.

The band members, of course, were neither barenaked nor ladies. They were an all-male satirical folk-rock combo from suburban Scarborough, fast gaining popularity for such songs as "The King of Bedside Manor" and "Be My Yoko Ono."

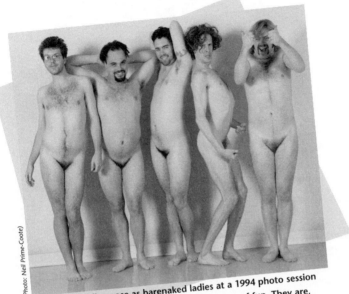

(Photo: Neil Prime-Coote)

Barenaked Ladies pose as barenaked ladies at a 1994 photo session that perfectly captures the Toronto band's sense of fun. They are, from left to right: Andy Creeggan, Tyler Stewart, Ed Robertson, Jim Creeggan and Steven Page.

"'Barenaked ladies' is children's language," lead singer Steven Page said in early January when news of the ban became public. The name was picked to suggest innocence and fun, he explained, in keeping with the band's humorous songs and goofy image.

On talk shows and in newspapers, the controversy raged for days.

"This is an example," stated one anonymous caller, "of why Toronto is known as a tight-assed conservative bore across the country and right around this world."

"Save us, City Hall!" *Sun* reader John Roff wrote sarcastically. "I've just discovered that if you play their music backwards, it repeats: 'Shop on Sunday, Shop on Sunday, Shop on Sunday.'"

"Boy, did I make a mistake," Chris Korwin-Kuczynski, a city councillor and chairman of the New Year's celebration, sheepishly admitted afterwards. But Mayor June Rowlands refused to lift the ban, inadvertently helping the group sell 85,000 copies of their first cassette tape, known as "the yellow cassette." It became the first independent release in the country to reach the charts, and the first to go gold.

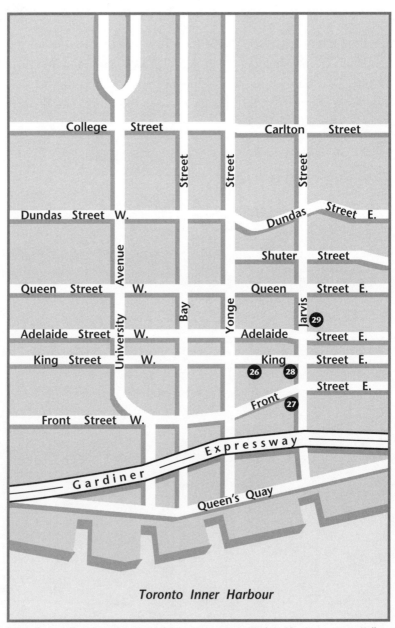

LEGEND: 26 – The King Edward Hotel; 27 – St. Lawrence Market; 28 – St. Lawrence Hall; 29 – The Jarvis House

26

The King Edward Hotel

37 KING STREET EAST

Before the King Edward opened in 1903, the city boasted no accommodations to which royalty and other high-ranking visitors could be directed without apology. New York had the Waldorf-Astoria. London had the Savoy. Montreal had the Windsor. The best Toronto could offer was Rossin House, at King and York Streets (since demolished), a prestigious enough building when it opened in 1856, but by the end of the century, desperately old-fashioned. Civic authorities saw a need for a hotel whose grandeur matched the status of the society and business clientele the city hoped to attract.

"What the Canadian Pacific Railway is to the country at large, the Kind Edward Hotel is to the city," a feature in the Toronto *Globe* stated as construction of the edifice neared completion in 1902. "The King Edward Hotel is by all odds the greatest commercial building in the Dominion."

The most rewarding view of the site today is from the northwest corner, at King and Victoria Streets. The vantage affords a good perspective of the Ionic columns said to emphasize the height and mass of the building, and, more important, offers a clear look at the grand bay window that graces the former vice-regal suite, on the eighth floor, one floor from the top. On each of three visits to the city – in 1964, 1965, and 1966 – the suite was rented to the Beatles, and on all three occasions, throngs of agitated teenage girls congregated beneath their window hoping to catch a glimpse of them.

Among the crowds more than once was Carolyn Smart, 13 years old when she first saw the Beatles in 1965. Now she is an accomplished poet, author, and professor of creative writing at Queen's University in Kingston, Ontario, but she remains a Beatles fan. She has kept all six Beatles scrapbooks she assembled as a young teenager, along with several fan magazines and a miniature yellow submarine that pops open to reveal John, Paul, George, and Ringo. Leafing through the memorabilia 30 years later, she recalls those manic days.

"I was 11 and in boarding school in England when the Beatles became famous, in 1963," she begins. "My older sister was a Rolling Stones fan, but the Stones were a little daunting to me at that age. They were a little scary. They were sexual, whereas the Beatles were sweeter, and I think that's what drew me to someone like Paul McCartney, my favorite Beatle at the time, who was very pretty, rather than to someone like John Lennon, who was much more handsome.

"I was still in England when the Beatles first came to Toronto in 1964, but the next year I was home and won tickets from CHUM. My sister and I sat in the front row on the left-hand side of the stage, right in front of Paul. We were literally, I would say, 20 feet from him. It was amazing.

"I remember we dressed in these little linen dresses, with stockings and proper shoes on – it was over 110 degrees in the Gardens – and when the Beatles came out it was like the Pope being carried into St. Peter's or something. There were so many flash bulbs going off, millions and millions and millions, and everyone just screaming and screaming. You couldn't hear a word the Beatles sang.

"This [a pulped gelatin mess on a scrapbook page] is a squashed jellybean. In those days, the Beatles used to get asked silly things in interviews like 'What's your favorite color?' or 'What do you like to snack on?' and one of them, I don't remember which one, said he liked jellybabies. So in North America, not having jellybabies, which are like jujubes, people brought jellybeans and threw them at the stage. They were all over the stage, and at the end of the show I went to the front and grabbed one that Paul had stepped on."

"The following year, 1966, the Beatles came back on the same date, August 17. They gave two concerts, afternoon and evening, and I went to both. That whole day was like an ultra-marathon. I weighed myself the night before and then the day after, and I lost seven pounds in one day, which shows the activity level that we were up to.

"I got up at 5 o'clock in the morning with my friend Cathy Baldwin, a girl I had met that summer at camp. She was staying with me in Forest Hill. We walked to the St. Clair subway station for when it opened at 6, and went down to King Street, to what was then called the King Edward Sheraton.

"When we got there we saw a crowd of, I would say, 40 or 50 young women outside, and we sang, 'We Love You Beatles' and all those things. We were really hoping that they would come to the window, but they didn't, and then I was worried that my mother didn't know where we were, so we went back home."

—

"Our tickets that year weren't particularly good. We were in the greens, but nevertheless, we were there, and we saw them. There were four of us [at the afternoon show], and right in the middle, Cathy Baldwin just suddenly flopped down at our feet. I suddenly remembered that something odd had happened at camp, which in retrospect I realize was an epileptic seizure, but I really had no idea what was going on. I just knew the St. John Ambulance people were kind of looking up at us – maybe they saw her fall, I don't know – and we were trying to keep her down so they wouldn't notice there might be a problem. We didn't want them to take her away and make her miss the concert."

—

(Photo: *Toronto Star*)

Carolyn Smart (circled, upper left) races after a police paddy wagon carrying the Beatles as they leave the King Edward Hotel on August 18, 1966. Joining the rush are her friends Liz Legge (centre) and Cathy Baldwin (lower left).

"This is a newspaper photograph of me chasing the Beatles' paddy wagon, taken the next day outside the King Eddie as they left for the airport. There was a very large crowd on the street, hundreds and hundreds of people, and I couldn't believe it was so easy to get close. I got out in front of everybody, and I could see George Harrison and Ringo Starr right through the tiny little cage at the back looking out – somewhat nervously – at this huge crowd. And

(Photo: Toronto Star)

Teenagers break through police lines outside the King Edward Hotel as they chase the departing Beatles on August 18, 1966. Circled at top right is Liz Legge.

I thought, 'I'm so close, I could actually jump on,' because by that point the policemen had got off and there was a clear way to hop on.

"Then suddenly I looked over my shoulder to see if my friends were near me. This [in the centre of the photo] is my closest friend in high school, Liz Legge. I looked to see if she was near me, and I saw about 10 or 12 mounted police charging down the road towards us, and I lost my nerve. I just pulled away. No one got on the paddy wagon. It just took off."

"After the Beatles left, Cathy Baldwin and I went back to the King Edward. There were lots of girls outside on King Street, but we walked in through a side door, and there was a clear-plastic box on the wall where people dropped their room keys before leaving. We reached in and took a key, so if anybody said to us, 'What are you doing here?' we'd say, 'We're guests at the hotel,' and flash the key.

"We didn't want to go straight into the lobby. We were sort of paranoid that we would be thrown out, because we didn't *look* like guests of the hotel, so we went up the back stairs. I think this is how all the weight poured off. We ran up and down the stairs it seemed

PAUL
STOOD
ON
THIS—
AUG.
17th, 1965.
9:00.

(Photo: John Goddard)

"This is a squashed jellybean," says Carolyn Smart, indicating a pulped gelatin mess on a scrapbook page. "At the end of the show, I went to the front and grabbed one that Paul had stepped on."

like for hours. We just had to move. It was like we were in this incredibly high-energy field and we couldn't stand still, we had to run everywhere, and finally we burst onto the eighth floor.

"The Beatles had all gone. We knew that. We just wanted to get into the room and see if we could find things, like used soap. I remember that there were these huge double doors. They were unlocked, and when we went inside there was a huge living-room and rooms off to the side.

"We didn't find any used soaps, but we found unused soaps. Here is the soap from Paul's bathroom. How we knew it was Paul's I don't remember. And there were cigarettes in the ashtray. We figured that the Beatles smoked Marlboros, because at one point we had seen a close-up photograph of Ringo smoking, and you could read 'Marlboro' around the cigarette. There were Marlboros in the ashtray, so we took the butts. We put them in our pockets. Those are the most exciting things we found. We also found a radio station pennant, and a fan letter from a hotel guest."

"This is a picture of one of our cakes. We used to make a cake every time any major event happened, like somebody's birthday, or when the Beatles came to town. Doris Cocomile and I would bake 20 cakes and put them together to make one huge cake, double-layered. The idea was to get some interest from a radio station, and be able to present the cake to the Beatles themselves.

"Here's a picture of some girls who got into the Beatles' press conference by petitioning the premier's office. They wrote to Premier John Robarts asking if he could arrange a meeting. The premier passed the letter along to a television show, *After Four*, with the explanation that the girls' problem was not exactly within the premier's sphere of responsibility, and *After Four* got them into the press conference. Their letter got action, you see. We were always hoping to be like them.

"On this cake we made a map of the world, putting in tiny flags, one for each country where the Beatles had been. Then we would take this down to the radio station, and normally we would have to leave it there, but one year [CHUM disc jockey] Bob McAdorey called us in for an interview. So we went in and he asked us why we were doing this, and we said that we loved the Beatles. He was really nice to us.

"But then the following morning – there used to be a character who

Beatles memorabilia from the scrapbooks of Carolyn Smart include: concert tickets; a photo of the band's hotel window; a CHUM Chart showing George, Paul, and John with disc jockey Jungle Jay Nelson; hotel soaps and stationery; and a photo of one of the gigantic cakes Smart baked with Doris Cocomile.

(Photo: John Goddard)

still does a kind of nasty news commentary on some of the soft-rock stations, and who did commentary on CHUM at that time. J.J. Richards. He was mean to us. He did this nasty reportage the following morning about how they had all been eating our cake in the CHUM cafeteria, and he broke his tooth on a jellybean. I mean, that wasn't our fault. He said that we were spoiled little girls, and we should be doing something better with our time."

"Liz Legge and I were actually Beatles fanatics all through our experience together. She was a big George Harrison fan, and as I grew up, I changed my allegiance from Paul to John, probably after Paul got married. In 1969, we went down to the Windsor Arms Hotel [at 22 St. Thomas Street] to try to see John and Yoko, who were on their peace campaign and who were staying there. I never really expected to see them, but I thought it would be nice enough to stand outside a building where we knew John was staying.

"So we were standing outside the Windsor Arms, it was raining slightly, there were two other young women there, and suddenly John and Yoko walked right out in front of us. I thought I was going to faint. Really, I did, I was completely overwhelmed by this enormous nausea.

(Photo: John Goddard)

Former Beatlemaniac Carolyn Smart looks over old scrapbooks at her home outside Kingston, Ontario. As a teenager, she once put her hands on John Lennon's shoulders.

"I thought, 'What can I do? What am I going to do?' And I started walking towards John with my arms extended. I was like a zombie. I got up to him, and I put my hands on his shoulders. He was wearing a white linen suit, and he was so thin that I could feel his shoulder blades through the padding. I leaned up to kiss him on the cheek. He sort of turned his face in my direction, and he said, 'Don't touch me, love,' and I fell back as if I had been wounded to the death. I kind of hung off to the side, stunned. It was one of those tunnel-vision moments. Then I saw Liz take from her handbag two wrapped presents, one for John and one for Yoko, and proceed to have this really fascinating conversation with them.

"She had been prepared. That's the kind of person she was. She had picked out presents – one was the love poems of Heloise and Abelard, which she gave to Yoko, and I forget what she gave John. They were beautifully wrapped and everything. I was so stunned.

"And Liz's parting line to John was, 'I think you're a desirable alien,' and he laughed. This was just after the U.S. government rejected him as an undesirable alien [because of a hashish conviction in Britain the year before]. Then he and Yoko got into a limousine and drove off.

"So Liz has had the high point of her life, and I've had the low point of my life. I said to Liz, 'Whaaaa, how did you do that?'

"She was really something. She later married a man called George who played guitar. My first husband, actually, was named John, and his birthday was on John Lennon's birthday."

27

St. Lawrence Market

91 FRONT STREET EAST

"It's got quite a high ceiling and it's all hard surfaces, so there is a natural reverberation to the space," says Loreena McKennitt about the enclosed entranceway to the St. Lawrence Market, at Front and Jarvis Streets. McKennitt ought to know. With her Celtic harp and cascading auburn hair, she cut a dramatic figure at the spot most Saturday mornings between 1986 and 1989, laying the groundwork for her startling rise as an international folk balladeer.

The space originally served as the foyer to Toronto's second city hall, completed in 1845. Spiral staircases once filled the room, leading upwards to a two-storey council chamber graced by elegant windows still visible from within the enclosed market centre, completed in 1901.

"The entranceway is ideal for busking," says McKennitt. "There are other spots, but they are noisier. Downstairs there is one major traffic spot that isn't desperately noisy, but in terms of major traffic and quiet and good sound, the front entrance is clearly the prize spot."

McKennitt grew up playing the piano and the guitar in Morden, Manitoba, near the North Dakota border. She moved to Winnipeg as a teenager in the mid-1970s, and after following a boyfriend to Ontario in 1981, she settled at Stratford, 90 miles west of Toronto. Later, she travelled to Ireland, and in 1985 recorded and produced *Elemental,* her own cassette of acoustically backed Celtic ballads.

The indie movement was dawning. Improved and cheaper recording technology was allowing musicians to produce their own independent cassette tapes. Marketing remained a problem, but McKennitt took guidance from a book called *How to Make and Sell Your Own Record,* by Diane Sward Rapaport of Arizona. "Know your audience," the book said, and McKennitt began commuting to the St. Lawrence Market to discover who might be drawn to her ethereal, vaguely melancholy sound.

"I would drive in on Saturday mornings, early, early, early in my little Civic," she recalls. "I pretty much had to be there by 6:30 to get the good spot, because there were certain gentlemen who knew it was a prime location for serious buskers. They would come along with a little mouth organ or whatever, and just kind of blow a couple of notes, but really they were there to be bought off by buskers such as myself. That's what would happen if I didn't get there early enough. So on the days I came in from Stratford, I would have to leave by four-thirty or five in the morning. At other times, I would drive in the night before and crash on somebody's couch."

The first hours would be slow, McKennitt says. People who arrive between 6 and 9 are serious shoppers. They don't hang around. Only after 9 a.m. do the more casual customers begin to drop by – people with families, and others who take pleasure in going to market on a Saturday morning. In the resonant entranceway, McKennitt would accompany herself on the harp for five or six songs, then stop for 15 or 20 minutes to talk to people, and maybe sell a cassette.

"It became a very social thing," she says. "I really loved meeting people week after week, a really diverse range of families and individuals. It was a very impor-

Doves alight around Loreena McKennitt's cascading auburn hair in a publicity photo accentuating her romantic image as a Celtic harpist. She is also a determined businesswoman who helped pioneer the recording and selling of independent cassette tapes.

(Photo: Pamela Betts)

tant time for me. I was able to develop confidence in the fact that there were people out there who were interested in my music, and the money allowed me to be independent, to build something for myself."

A good weekend could bring $600 to $800, she says. In warm weather she would appear at the market on Saturdays, and at York Quay, behind Harbourfront, on Sundays. She would also take names and addresses of people who stopped to listen, developing a mailing list through which she began to market her cassettes.

In 1987, McKennitt produced a second one, *To Drive the Cold Winter Away,* of particularly early folk tunes from the British Isles. Two years later she released a third, *Parallel Dreams,* in which she extended the early tunes in a subtly rock-driven way that distinguished her as a highly original artist. It led to her breakthrough. Warner Music signed her, and she quickly became Warner's top-selling Canadian artist worldwide. "It's almost a classic story of what any independent-label artist should do," the guidebook author, Rapaport, said at the time.

McKennitt has gone on to record several more albums, broadening her range to include north African sounds, or what she jokingly refers to as "Moroccan Roll." She has not entirely let go of the indie identity she formed at St. Lawrence Market, however. In her contract with Warner, she insisted on retaining rights to her Quinlan Road label and its mail-order distribution out of Stratford.

28

St. Lawrence Hall

157 KING STREET EAST

When tickets went on sale at nearby Nordheimer's Music Store, police had to barricade the building to keep back the crowds. All seats sold within two hours. After years of acclaim throughout Europe and Scandinavia, Jenny Lind, "the Swedish Nightingale," was coming to Toronto as part of a 93-date tour of North America, organized by showman P.T. Barnum. Hailed as the greatest vocal artist of her era, the star soprano packed St. Lawrence Hall for two shows on October 21 and 22, 1851.

In the same hall 120 years later, the first Canadian music awards were presented – the Juno Awards. The date was February 22, 1971. The hall swarmed with what the *Globe and Mail* described as "a large audience of long-haired musicians, medium hairy public-relations men, and balding vice-presidents of record companies." They had plenty to celebrate. For the first time, Canadian records were scoring major international hits.

The Guess Who, of Winnipeg, won the Juno for best group, having posted three hit singles the previous year: "Hand Me Down World," "No Time," and the hugely successful "American Woman" – the first Canadian-produced record ever to reach number 1 on the U.S. *Billboard* charts. Gordon Lightfoot won for top male vocalist with "If You Could Read My Mind," also an international seller. Bruce Cockburn took the Juno for best folk singer with the soundtrack to a landmark Canadian feature film, *Goin' Down the Road.* Anne Murray won for best female vocalist with her first international hit, "Snowbird."

"I remember the very first awards," Murray said as host of the silver-anniversary awards ceremony in 1996, broadcast live to a national television audience from Copps Coliseum in neighboring Hamilton. "As I recall, the room cleared out at midnight and we all took the subway home."

29

The Jarvis House

99 JARVIS STREET

The building stands abandoned now, with torn posters flapping from the lowest of its boarded windows, but once it housed a small, shabby club called the Jarvis House, where Bryan Adams performed on his twenty-first birthday.

Originally, the building was called Blair's Hotel, opened in 1859 by John Blair at what was then the heart of downtown. He subsequently died, and in 1875, Malcolm Macfarlane took over, renaming it Macfarlane's Hotel. Then Macfarlane died, and in 1898 his widow, Mary, had the place almost completely rebuilt into the three-storey establishment of decorative buff brickwork that survives today. Recently, the Toronto Historical Board named it a heritage site.

When Adams performed there on November 5, 1981, he was virtually unknown – far from the world fame that was to come with his 1991 rock ballad "(Everything I Do) I Do It For You," which set

(Photo: John Goddard)

Bryan Adams waves on his way into Edwards Books & Art (since closed), at 356 Queen Street West, during a snowy day in November, 1995. Stepping from the car in the background is his manager, Bruce Allen.

an all-time sales record for a song by a single artist. His self-titled first album had fared so badly that he wanted to call the second one *Bryan Adams Hasn't Heard of You, Either.* Instead, he called the album *You Want It, You Got It* and waited to see if anybody wanted it, or not.

To help promote the release, A&M Records arranged a media showcase in Toronto at the El Mocambo Tavern. Backing Adams were four players scrounged from Vancouver's top bar bands: Keith Scott on guitar, John Hannah on keyboards, Dave Reimer on bass, and Jim Wesley on drums. They were well received, and stayed to play several small clubs as well as a private party at Casa Loma, the 98-room hilltop mansion at 1 Austin Terrace, now one of the city's top tourist attractions. They recorded three songs there for an extended-play record called *You Want It, You Got It – Live.*

"The irony to me," says Keith Sharp, then a reporter for *Music Express* and later editor and publisher of *Access* magazine, "is that such a big fuss was made over the album launch at the ElMo, which was a Monday or a Tuesday, something like that. Then a couple of nights afterwards, the band was playing down at this little dive, the Jarvis House, to 30 or 40 people who didn't have a clue, really, who he was."

Sharp had already caught Adams several times during the stay, and ventured down to the Jarvis House with another *Music Express* staffer, Kandice Abbot. Sharp describes what happened next.

"We just went down basically to see him in a less formal situation [than the launch party]. We came in. We watched his set. The band played in a little corner, on a bit of a riser, and people were sitting around drinking. When he finished, we went over and signalled to him that we were there. We started chatting about the week, and he said, 'Hey, why don't you come upstairs and have a drink with me?'

"And I said, 'Oh – really?'

"He said, 'Yeah, we've got to celebrate.'

"I said, 'What are you celebrating?'

"He said, 'My twenty-first birthday.'

"So we were sitting – I'll never forget – at the top of these stairs, and just sort of looking down at the little area where you played. And I felt sorry for him. It was weird because there was nobody really to celebrate with him, just us and his band. It was one of those moments where you kind of got a feel for what it's like – you know, the band against the world kind of thing."

A fan bows to Bryan Adams during a packed autograph session on Queen Street West, as manager Bruce Allen (left) hovers nearby. Adams, who played at the Jarvis House on his twenty-first birthday in 1981, was back to sign copies of a glossy new photo book, *Bryan Adams*.

(Photo: John Goddard)

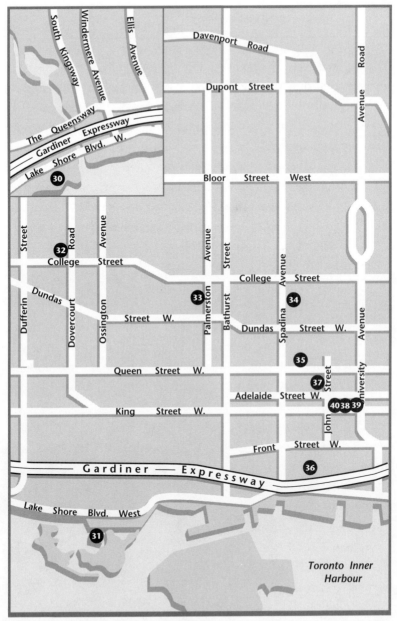

LEGEND: 30 – Seahorse Motel; 31 – Ontario Place Forum; 32 – The Matador Club; 33 – 256 Palmerston Avenue; 34 – Grossman's Tavern; 35 – The Horseshoe Tavern; 36 – The SkyDome; 37 – National Film Board; 38 – Royal Alexandra Theatre; 39 – The Pretzel Bell; 40 – Peermusic Canada Inc.

30 Seahorse Motel

2095 LAKE SHORE BOULEVARD WEST

The Seahorse Motel commands a scenic lakeshore site in west Toronto at the mouth of the Humber River. More important than the actual lakeshore to most guests, however, are Lake Shore Boulevard and the Gardiner Expressway. Vacationers choose the Seahorse for its convenience to downtown in one direction and to Niagara Falls and Canada's Wonderland in the other.

In 1964, Levon and the Hawks similarly found the motel handy when playing clubs downtown, or in Hamilton and London. The Hawks were the hottest band in Ontario at the time, freshly split from their former leader, Ronnie Hawkins, and a year or so away from joining Bob Dylan and becoming the Band. To them, the motel served both as a refuge from fans they did not want to see and as a place to which they could bring fans they had more time for, such as Cathy Evelyn Smith.

It was at the Seahorse Motel, a few weeks shy of her seventeenth birthday, that Smith began her spectacular career as one of rock music's most notorious groupies. At her peak, she lived with the Rolling Stones; at her nadir, she faced a second-degree murder charge in connection with the drug-overdose death of comedian and Blues Brother John Belushi. "I didn't kill John Belushi," she writes in her 1984 biography, *Chasing the Dragon.* "I want to tell my side of things as honestly as I can."

Smith got a tough start in life. She was born to an unwed mother in 1947 and was given up for adoption within six weeks. Her adoptive mother was a former circus showgirl, her adoptive father a logger-turned-cement-salesman. They lived west of Toronto, in Burlington. Both drank heavily, and for 10 years the mother was in and out of hospitals for depression. Sometimes she would threaten to send her daughter back where she came from.

"I had visions of having come out of a shoebox," Smith writes. "On the shelves [of my closet] were all my Barbie and Ken dolls – just like babies waiting to be adopted. Or just like bad babies who had been returned."

In the early 1960s, while Smith was in her early teens, she started listening to the Everly Brothers and Elvis Presley. She liked the physical side of music, she says. She liked to dance and felt attracted to energetic performers, especially drummers. Her first boyfriend was a drummer, and on her sixteenth birthday she quit school to chase other musicians. A few months later, at the Grange Tavern in nearby Hamilton, she met Levon and the Hawks for the first time.

"I walked in ... dressed to kill," she says without irony. She was also dressed to look 21, the legal drinking age at the time. She wore white lipstick, fishnet stockings, a tight red-and-black dress slit up the back, and teased hair blasted with Final Net hairspray. Once past the doorman, she and her best friend, Joyce Ivall, ordered rum-and-Cokes, and Ivall introduced Smith to the band. Smith liked Levon Helm best. Besides being the drummer, he was also the eldest of the group and the only non-Canadian – a 26-year-old from Arkansas.

"His southern accent charmed me," she writes. "Nobody drawls in Burlington."

Soon Smith was attending the band's shows regularly in Hamilton and Toronto. She became a groupie, and from the start she displayed the degrading lack of discrimination and self-respect that was to mark the whole of her 20-year career in the reflected glory of rock celebrity.

"One night a few months after I met them," she says of the Hawks, "they rented a few rooms in the Seahorse Motel down on the lakeshore. We partied on into the night, and at one point I ended up in bed with [bass guitarist] Rick Danko. In the middle of making love, Rick found out I wasn't on the pill and things (as it were) ground to a halt. He got out of bed and wandered on down the hall, leaving me lying there hurt and confused. Then Levon walked into the room [and] climbed into bed with me."

Six weeks later, Smith discovered she was pregnant. Levon was the father, she insists, although she also says that she "didn't belong particularly to Levon." Richard Manuel, the piano player, offered to marry her, but she turned him down. She loved only Helm, she says, and after giving birth to a daughter, she pursued him for months, trying to persuade him to acknowledge paternity.

He never did. Smith says that over the years, they continued to go to bed together occasionally, but in his own autobiography, *This Wheel's on Fire,* Helm assigns the relationship no importance. He mentions Smith only once, only by her first name (which he misspells as "Kathy"), and only in an anecdote told mostly by Rick Danko. In the summer of 1965, Helm says, the RCMP stopped the Hawks as they returned briefly to Canada from the United States. The police found marijuana between the car seats and in Danko's shirt pocket. Charges were laid, and the arresting officer appeared intent on sending all five band members to jail. Helm lets Danko tell the rest.

"So Levon spoke to this chick he was dating," Danko says. "Her name was Kathy and she was the most beautiful girl in Toronto ... [She] was 16 years old when we met her, and she was a gorgeous, gorgeous lady. She looked beautiful, and no one could resist her. Anyway, Levon explained the situation to her, and she kindly gave this cop who was trying to crucify us a blow job. Then she told him she was 14 years old. He was the chief witness against us, but this was some weird shit for him, and he disappeared, we never saw him again. In the end everyone else got off, and I received a year's suspended sentence on probation."

Smith, in her book, gives her own version of the event. "At first I couldn't believe that they would ask me to do something like that – but I was their friend and I wanted to help them out," she writes. "Ridiculous as it sounds, it seemed logical at the time, and I didn't see how I was being used until later."

After the Hawks left town with Dylan in 1965, Smith gave up her baby for adoption. She took a waitressing job at the Riverboat coffeehouse at 134 Yorkville Avenue, the pre-eminent folk club in the country, and began to cut a wide swath through the entertainment crowd. She lists a number of major and minor conquests, including a four-year on-and-off affair with Gordon Lightfoot as his career was taking off. "The greatest romance of my life," she calls it, although she also says that Lightfoot was married at the time, that she herself got married to and divorced from somebody else during the affair, and that they expressed intense feelings for each other almost exclusively through drunken sex and physical violence.

In 1974, she upped the ante and moved to California. Hoyt Axton, a Los Angeles–based singer-songwriter and longtime cocaine addict (and composer of the drug song "The Pusher," made famous by Steppenwolf), hired her as a "backup singer" – meaning, she says, "live-in playmate." Two years later she rejoined the Band for their

Last Waltz, and in 1978 she house-sat in Los Angeles for Rolling Stones guitarist Ron Wood, sharing quarters at one point with Keith Richards. Smith had climbed to the pinnacle of rock and roll, but working for the Stones, she says, drove her to heroin.

"Although I didn't reflect on it at the time, I was dealing with my own perverse brand of 'success,'" she writes. "With the Stones I was at the top, as far as vicarious living went. But in terms of my own life, my own sense of who I was, I was nowhere."

Smith's contribution to rock-and-roll literature lies not so much in critical analysis, as in her unique access and in her eye for sordid detail. She liked to shower with celebrities, and tells what she discovered about them under the faucet. Gordon Lightfoot always wore a rubber glove on his left hand to protect the callouses on his fingertips. Keith Richards "didn't have big railroad tracks down his arms," despite his heroin habit, she also discovered. "He only injected himself in his muscles. There was a spot on his biceps where you could see where the needle had gone, but that was all."

Richard Manuel looked terrible when naked, she says. "When he took off his clothes you could see his liver – literally see his liver – bulging out of his belly. His skin was so saturated with alcohol that it drooped over his muscles. I had the feeling that if I pressed my thumb against it, it would leave an impression forever."

Smith's glory days ended at the Chateau Marmont hotel in Los Angeles on March 5, 1982, when John Belushi was found dead of a heroin and cocaine overdose. Smith had been the last person to see him alive. Police charged her with second-degree murder.

"What happened to me could happen to anyone," she says in her book, written in Toronto while awaiting trial. In a California courtroom, however, she confessed to administering the overdose that killed Belushi. She pleaded guilty to a lesser charge of involuntary manslaughter, and served 18 months of a three-year sentence.

31

Ontario Place Forum

955 LAKE SHORE BOULEVARD WEST

"I remember going there," says Gordon Lewis, the lead guitarist for Teenage Head. "I took the subway. I was by myself. I had my guitar in my hand, and when I arrived I was kind of looking to find the dressing room or someplace. I was walking through the stands – this was about 4 o'clock – and there were people there. That's when I got a sense that something unusual was happening – people were there at 4 o'clock for an 8 o'clock show."

Lewis is talking about the concert of June 2, 1980, at the Ontario Place Forum, where fans rioted and turned Teenage Head into the most feared and the most sought-after rock band in the country. The group consisted of Gordon Lewis on lead guitar, Steve Marshall on bass, Nick Stipanitz on drums, and on vocals, Frank Kerr – better known as Frankie Venom, an exuberant, reckless, unpredictable performer who perfectly expressed the spirit of freedom-seeking and youth rebellion at the core of early rock and roll.

The attention was a long time coming. The members first met in the early 1970s at Westdale Secondary School, west of Toronto in Hamilton. They formed a garage band, rejecting disco and the overblown "progressive rock" popular at the time, to embrace a more stripped-down, elemental form. They identified with Eddie Cochran's rudimentary guitar sounds and Gene Vincent' s whooping vocal style. They listened to early Elvis, Buddy Holly, Chuck Berry, and some of the 1960s' precursors to punk rock such as Velvet Underground, MC5, and Iggy Pop and the Stooges. "We were listening to music everyone else was throwing away," drummer Stipanitz once said.

In 1975, punk rock's immediate progenitors, the New York Dolls, came to Toronto. Lewis and Marshall went to see them at the Queensbury Arms, at Eglinton Avenue and Weston Road. The Dolls proved a revelation. With their lipstick and fishnet stockings, and taste for the same kind of raw, energized doo-wop that Teenage Head liked so much, the Dolls showed that it was possible to go against dominant trends and create a following.

"We nursed one beer the whole night and had a great time," Lewis says. "We were only 18 or 19. I knew this was where we fit in, and it felt really nice to fit in, because when we were playing this music in Hamilton, we felt that we didn't."

At around the same time, the band discovered an emerging musical underground in Toronto. Teenage Head's introduction to it, Lewis says, came with a concert billed as the 3-D Show at the Ontario College of Art, featuring the Diodes, the Dishes, and the Doncasters. "That's where I first met Steve Leckie," he says. "He had Nazi Dog and the Viletones, but he hadn't had a gig yet. We were the same. We didn't have gigs either, but we were telling everybody about this band we had. 'Yeah,' we said, 'we got a band called Teenage Head.'

"After that," Lewis continues, "Leckie started to branch out. He wanted to get his band playing, and he basically founded the

Colonial Underground, just a basement underneath the Colonial Tavern [at 201–203 Yonge Street]. That's where he played his first show with the Viletones. We went to that, and we asked for a gig there, too. And they said, 'Okay, you're booked. You can play.'"

In September 1976, the Ramones came to Toronto for the first time. They were among the leaders of the emerging New York underground centred at CBGB, the Bowery bar where such raw new acts as Talking Heads, Suicide, Patti Smith, and Blondie (with Debbie Harry) were appearing. The Ramones were the first of them to take their act internationally – to London, then to Toronto. "We booked them at the New Yorker Theatre [at 651 Yonge Street]," recalls the show's Toronto promoter, Gary Topp, "and there wasn't a heck of a big scene for that kind of music at the time. The theatre held 500 people, and we did about 1,000 people over the three nights."

Despite the moderate turnout, the Ramones conferred a legitimacy on the local underground movement that led to the next landmark event the following spring on May 27, 1977. Promoter Ralph Alfonso and his friends, the Diodes, opened a basement punk club at 15 Duncan Street, behind the Royal Alexandra Theatre. They named it the Crash 'n' Burn, and it is remembered now as the high point of the local punk era.

"The Crash 'n' Burn – that's when I noticed that the thing was growing

(Photo: Tom Rabe)

Sassy even in repose, Teenage Head vocalist Frankie Venom (centre) takes a break during rehearsals at the Crash 'n' Burn club in the summer of 1977, while guitarist Gordon Lewis (left) runs through his licks. "As things fell apart in one place, we just kind of moved to another," Lewis recalls.

and growing," says Lewis. "It was only one summer. You'd think it lasted a year or something, but it was only the summer of '77. The thing went from May to September, if that, but the Crash 'n' Burn was when the suburban kids caught on, and when international bands were dropping by. I remember Thin Lizzy were playing in town, and they dropped by. The Ramones would come to town and they would drop by. By the time we played there it was on its way out. Our show was packed but the club had lost its liquor licence, and as things fell apart in one place we just kind of moved to another one, like Larry's Hideaway [at 121 Carlton Street], which was definitely a showcase for all the punk bands. I remember playing there one night when Blondie was at Ontario Place, and the whole band came down to Larry's after and played a song."

On December 2, 1978, the city's punk era officially ended. The leading bands congregated at the Horseshoe Tavern for a show called the Last Pogo, starring Teenage Head. It was both a celebration and a recognition that punk had run its course. By then, however, Teenage Head was proving more than just a punk band. Their stage shows still centred on Frankie Venom's climbing dangerously up microphone stands and tossing himself bodily into crowds, but the band was also playing highly danceable music of the type that had

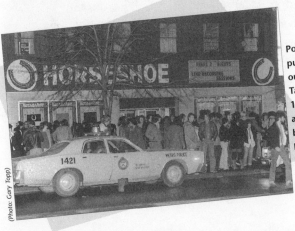

(Photo: Gary Topp)

Police keep an eye on punk fans congregating outside the Horseshoe Tavern on December 2, 1978, for the Last Pogo, a roundup of local punk bands starring Teenage Head. The show was both a celebration and a recognition that punk rock had run its course.

made rock and roll popular and broadly commercial in the first place.

"We have a wide cross-section of fans now," drummer Stipanitz said at the time. "We get the punk and new-wave fans, but there's also some heavy-metal fans and the bopper crowd in our audiences. Our musical

A hoarding on Queen Street West in 1977 displays posters for punk-music events, including a return engagement of the Ramones at the New Yorker Theatre, and a Diodes' show at the Crash 'n' Burn.

(Photo: Tom Robe)

direction has changed a bit. All of us have huge record collections and we like to try different styles, add some variety. It's been a natural progression, and we're learning to play better as we go along. We've been called punk and new wave, but all along it's really been basic rock and roll. We've just kept the attitude of punk – kept the energy and the 'anything goes' feeling."

All through 1979, Teenage Head played clubs and hockey arenas across southern Ontario and the rest of the country. They released their first album, *Teenage Head,* which critics knocked for its production values but praised for its fast, entertaining songs – particularly the single "Top Down."

In April 1980, they released their second album, *Frantic City.* It was a breakthrough, featuring such irrepressible tunes as "Let's Shake," Infected," and "Disgusteen." Reviewers called it "explosive" and "like a lightning bolt," and it was just starting to get airplay when the band announced that on June 2 they would play at Ontario Place

Forum. Hoping to arouse interest south of the border, they also invited label representatives from New York and music directors from several U.S. radio stations.

The Forum was an outdoor amphitheatre. It stood on the smallest and most central of three artificial islands that make up Ontario Place, the waterfront entertainment park west of downtown. Until the Molson Amphitheatre replaced it in 1995, the Forum served for more than 20 years as the city's premier summer concert venue.

The venue featured a circular revolving stage, sheltered by a roof, and open at the sides. Surrounding the stage was bench seating for 2,500 people. Beyond the benches stretched grassy hills offering places to sit for another 8,000 people, or more if squeezed together, putting a capacity crowd at between 10,500 and 12,000 people.

Entrance to the Forum was free with park admission. Access was via four bridges. Security depended largely on the location's relaxed summer atmosphere and the co-operative attitudes of Toronto audiences. Few problems ever surfaced, but six days before Teenage Head's scheduled appearance, trouble developed among a crowd leaving a Forum show featuring local bands Goddo, and Nash the Slash. Fans on their way home kept pouring off streetcars at Bathurst subway station, but no subway trains were arriving to pick them up. A crowd of 1,500 people collected, and when a train finally arrived, some fans started kicking over garbage cans, smashing windows, and ripping up seats. Damage was estimated at $5,500. As a precaution for the Teenage Head show, 75 police officers were assigned to the bridge gates. Hundreds of others prepared to monitor streetcar and subway points.

On the afternoon of June 2, as Lewis witnessed, fans began to gather early. By evening, they were converging on the site by the thousand. A full hour before showtime, the crowd stood at 12,500 people, exceeding maximum official capacity, and hundreds more continued to pour through the main park entrances, paying full admission. By the time "sold out" signs could be posted, 1,500 paying spectators found themselves being barred from the island by police.

Most of the trouble started at the east bridge. About 400 people stormed the chain-link fence, some fans hurling bottles and rocks. The police hit out with nightsticks. One youth jumped into the water to dodge an officer's stick, inspiring others to dive in and swim to the Forum side, adding to the general chaos.

Onstage, unaware of trouble, the band members charged into one of their wildest shows ever. It was Frankie Venom's birthday – his twenty-fourth – and pumped by the crowd, he leapt madly around the stage, more than once tossing himself into the front rows with abandon. "The best rock and roll Toronto has seen all year," reported *Toronto Sun* reviewer Jonathan Gross.

One fan clambered to the rooftop to moon spectators on the hill-sides. Other people lit firecrackers, sparklers, and massive bonfires on the grass. The most frenzied fans rushed the stage, nearly tackling Venom more than a dozen times, and when the band came out for an encore, the crowd broke loose.

"We had to stop the show," Lewis says. "We came back on and people started running all over the place. It reminded me of the Beatles at Shea Stadium, people running onto the stage and running off. It doesn't happen too often, that's why I remember it so well. I remember running just to get off, and somebody snatching one of my guitars. A roadie had to chase a guy halfway up the stands to get it back."

Numbers tell part of the story. Arrests: 58. Quantity of wine, beer and liquor seized: 225 gallons. Injuries: 10 officers and several fans hurt, none seriously. Police cruisers trashed: one. Police cruisers partly damaged: two. Number of newspapers in Canada playing the story on page 1: 93. Number of rock concerts allowed at the Forum for the rest of the summer: zero.

In the week following the show, *Frantic City* sold 10,000 copies. Later in the summer, nervous organizers cancelled a Teenage Head show at the Canadian National Exhibition, creating even greater demand. Invitations arrived from New York. Showcase dates were booked for early September, beginning at My Father's Place on Long Island, to be broadcast live on radio station WLIR-FM. Friday- and Saturday-night appearances were scheduled at The '80s club in Manhattan, with more than 100 record-company people, celebrities, and reporters representing every rock magazine from *New York Rocker* to *Rolling Stone* expected to attend. Similar dates were arranged for the following month in Hollywood.

For Teenage Head, the big break had arrived, but two days before their planned departure for New York, Lewis landed in the hospital. On the way back from a show in Palmerston, Ontario, the van in which Lewis and Marshall were travelling crashed headlong into a ditch. A security guard was driving. Marshall was unhurt, but Lewis ended up in "serious but stable condition," with a back injury and broken ribs.

The band cancelled the New York shows immediately. They hung on to the Hollywood dates for a while, but in the end had to cancel them as well. Five months later, in mid-February, Lewis recovered enough to return to the stage, but by then the buzz had died. Agents and talent scouts had moved on, and Teenage Head never got a second chance.

But they are still together. With Mark Lockerbie replacing Stipanitz on drums, Teenage Head continues to play gritty, unrestrained rock and roll every weekend in clubs around southern Ontario and other parts of the country to a loyal and ardent following. Critics still cite *Frantic City* as one of the best Canadian rock-and-roll albums of all time.

32 The Matador Club

466 DOVERCOURT ROAD

"It's real, it's straight up, and it's a little wacky," Johnny Lovesin says of the Matador, where for years he served as leader of the house band. "Walk through the door and you could be in Sudbury, Thunder Bay, Saskatoon – anywhere but Toronto."

The club was built as a dance hall during World War I, and was being used as a bowling alley when the current owners, Ann Dunn and her daughter Charmaine, first saw it in 1964. They bought it, stripped it to the original hardwood floor, and redesigned the place as an after-hours honky-tonk open every Friday and Saturday night from 1 a.m. Since then, for more than 30 years, they have played host to bikers, rounders, inveterate night-owls, and anybody else who appreciates country music in a down-home setting. "We'll never have line dancing here," says Ann. "It looks dumb."

One fan of the place is Leonard Cohen. His first visit came early one morning in 1970, when Charmaine spotted him in Yorkville and coaxed him back for a guest appearance. "I hadn't heard of him," Ann says, "but Charmaine told me he'd been the highest-paid artist at the Isle of Wight Festival in England. Well, that meant he must be some good. He went on and kind of mumbled, but he was a presence."

In November 1992, Cohen returned to the club to shoot a video for "Closing Time," his country-style hit song about drinking, dancing, and "Johnnie Walker wisdom running high." The Matador must have struck him as the perfect backdrop, with its barnwood panelling in the lobby, and kitschy handout photos of country-music singers on the walls. To heighten the effect, the director hired 100 extras to mill around – men in skinny neckties, women in tight dresses and platinum beehives.

Cohen's girlfriend of the time was there as well, actress Rebecca De Mornay, fresh from her role as the deranged nanny in *The Hand That Rocks the Cradle*. She was in a playful mood, as writer Ian Pearson witnessed while on assignment for *Saturday Night* magazine.

As Cohen lip-synched to the music, Pearson writes, De Mornay began to dance seductively beside the camera. "Oh we're drinking and we're dancing …," Cohen mouthed as De Mornay began to grind. "And my very close companion gets me fumbling …," he mimed as she ran her fingers along the edges of her lips. "And the women tear their blouses off …," he pretended to sing as she moved her hands suggestively in front of her breasts, causing Cohen's moody countenance to dissolve into an intensely erotic gaze.

33

256 Palmerston Avenue

Percy Faith began playing the violin at age 7 and the piano at 10. He was a child prodigy. At 11 he got a job playing piano in silent-movie houses, and at 14 he played Massey Hall for the first time, as a student of the Toronto Conservatory of Music. Bursting with talent, he seemed destined for a brilliant concert career. Then disaster struck.

"Our 5-year-old sister found some matches," recalls Ruth Stanleigh, who was 6 at the time. "She thought she'd light them so other children wouldn't get hurt. That's what she said. She thought it was the right thing to do."

It was the summer of 1926. The Faiths lived at 256 Palmerston – not on the grand stretch between College and Bloor Streets known as Palmerston Boulevard, with stone gates at each end, but along the quainter section south of College called Palmerston Avenue, in

Percy Faith, one of pop's most versatile musicians, sits at a piano shortly before his death from cancer in 1976. In an unselfish act of heroism when he was a teenager, Faith ended his hopes for a concert career while saving his sister's life.

a squarish two-storey semi-detached house. There were eight children in the family. Ruth was the sixth child, the girl playing with matches, the seventh. Percy, the eldest, was 18 years old and still a student at the Conservatory. He was working on a music score in his bedroom when the match ignited.

"Being so young," Ruth continues, "our sister let the fire catch on her dress. She was wearing one of these flimsy dresses that we wear in summer, and it caught quickly."

Suddenly, Percy heard terrible screams. He rushed into the hallway in time to see the girl hurtling towards him in a ball of flames. Instinctively, he reached to smother them, saving his sister's life but burning his own hands so badly that his hopes for a concert career ended. His doctor told him not even to touch a piano for five years.

"I hate even to talk about it," Ruth says of the fire. "Our sister almost died. She was in the hospital for 18 months, and in those days there were no burn units. She suffered a great deal."

Percy rebounded from his own injuries to study theory and composition under the renowned teacher Louis Waizman, a former Austrian violinist. Soon Percy was writing arrangements for hotel-orchestra leaders Luigi Romanelli (at the King Edward) and Rex Battle (at the Royal York). He then went into radio work as a composer, arranger, and conductor, and by 1938 he had his own CBC Radio show, *Music by Faith,* also carried on stations south of the border.

In 1940, his big break came. The U.S. radio exposure landed him a job at NBC radio in Chicago, where he conducted the *Contented Hour* radio series and began his steady rise to the forefront of American popular music. Ten years later he became pop-music director at Columbia Records, working first in New York until 1959, then in Los Angeles until his death from cancer, in early 1976, at age 67.

Faith is remembered as one of the best studio arrangers in the business and as the conductor of one of the few easy-listening string orchestras that also managed to swing. His legacy at Columbia includes 45 record albums. With his own arrangements and compositions, he helped launch Tony Bennett and Guy Mitchell as popular singers, and with his own orchestra and chorus he recorded a string of hits, including "Delicado," a number 1 single in 1952, and "Song from Moulin Rouge," the top-selling single of 1953. Two years later, he drew an Oscar nomination for his first movie score, for *Love Me or Leave Me,* starring Doris Day. He also won two Grammys – one in 1969 for "Love Theme from *Romeo and Juliet,*" the other in 1960 for the movie score that most made him famous, "Theme from *A Summer Place.*"

Written by Max Steiner, and performed by Percy Faith and His Orchestra, the song complemented the film, a romantic melodrama set on the coast of Maine, starring Troy Donahue and Sandra Dee. The tune also spent 17 weeks on the *Billboard* Hot 100 chart, including nine weeks at the top spot. Sales of more than two million copies made it the top-selling single of 1960.

Steiner earned a Grammy nomination for the composition. Faith won for record of the year, beating out Elvis Presley ("Are You

Lonesome Tonight"), Ella Fitzgerald ("Mack the Knife"), Frank Sinatra ("Nice 'n' Easy"), and Ray Charles ("Georgia on My Mind").

"He was a wonderful, sweet man," says Ruth Stanleigh, who saw her brother often on his trips back to Canada. He was also one of the most accomplished and versatile pop musicians of his time.

34

Grossman's Tavern

377 SPADINA AVENUE

Grossman's Tavern is the blues joint where Dan Aykroyd made his first bumbling attempts at playing a Blues Brother.

The club's beginnings date to the early 1950s, when a local entrepreneur named Al Grossman knocked the first-floor interiors out of an old double house on Spadina Avenue, south of College Street, and opened a restaurant called Grossman's Cafeteria. In 1957, he obtained a liquor licence that allowed the eatery to evolve into the first drinking spot in the city to serve draft beer in pitchers. Later, he added live music.

Little about Grossman's has changed since. Al sold the tavern in 1975 and later died, but the new manager of more than 20 years, Christina Louie, continues both the name and the neighborhood blues-bar tradition, hiring local bands that attract a mix of students and old-timers. Outside, mint-green siding has been added, and signs marking the Century 21 realty office upstairs make the building appear perpetually for sale, but inside it is still the same homey, beer-drenched, dimly lit establishment, divided by the original super-structure and featuring a cafeteria-style counter along one wall. Over the bar at the back hangs a recent award from *Now* magazine for "Best Blues Bar" in the city.

Several well-known acts trace their roots to Grossman's. Alannah Myles, Rough Trade, and the Jeff Healey Band all started at the tavern, and in 1995 the Jeff Healey Band returned to record their third album, *Cover to Cover,* live over two nights. In Grossman's lore, however, one group looms above all others: the Downchild Blues Band, featuring Donnie Walsh on lead guitar and harmonica, and his younger brother Richard on vocals.

Donnie was the ostensible leader of the group. He named himself "Mr. Downchild" after a Sonny Boy Williamson song, and then named the group after himself. Standing tall and lean, he played guitar with an uncommon sense of swing that informed the band's entire sound – jumped-up Chicago-style blues punctuated by a trumpet and by tenor, alto, and baritone saxophones.

Richard goes by "Hock," a nickname derived from his steady diet of pork hocks when they sold for 18 cents a pound. Relatively short, mop-haired, and roly-poly, he wooed audiences with his bluesy feel and uncommon vocal range. Together, Donnie and Richard Walsh were the blues brothers, although they never went by that name.

"When I first knew Grossman's in the mid-sixties," says Hock, "the blacks sat along the south wall, the Portuguese along the north wall, and they fought each other. To settle things down, Al started bringing in Hungarian bands, but that only clashed with everybody's taste in music and became a source of fights as well. So Al decided, 'No more bands.' Then in June 1969, he made a decision to hire a blues band – us."

Until then the group had played a total of two afternoon performances. At Grossman's, they played six nights a week for the next two years. Their payment came first from passing the hat. Then, in January 1970, Grossman started paying them a regular wage – "$20 per man, per week, per haps," Hock says. Later, the band took extra dates in other clubs, sometimes performing six evening shows, three matinées, and three after-hours jobs in a single week. "By 1972–73, our itineraries were crazy," he says. "I remember working Grossman's and Egerton's the same night – a seven-piece band and two sets of equipment riding back and forth in cabs."

They were working hard, and through the early 1970s, they were making a name for themselves as a tight, entertaining blues band. In 1971 they released their first album, *Bootleg,* followed in 1973 by perhaps their all-time best record, *Straight Up,* containing the Canadian hit single "Flip, Flop and Fly."

Dan Aykroyd started to drop by Grossman's sometime in the early 1970s. Aykroyd, who is from Ottawa, was working in the Second City comedy troupe at the Old Firehall, at 110 Lombard Street, a dozen or so blocks east. He would finish at around 11:30 p.m. and be at Grossman's sometime after midnight. Often, he would get up to play harmonica with Donnie.

(Photo: Jann Van Horne)

Richard "Hock" Walsh shows his comic side during a performance at the Isabella Hotel on Sherbourne Street in 1981. With their performances at Grossman's Tavern, he and his brother, Donnie, inspired the Blues Brothers sketch by comedians Dan Aykroyd and John Belushi.

"He couldn't play harmonica to save his life," Hock recalls dryly, "but then neither could Donnie – not then."

By the fall of 1977, Aykroyd had moved to New York. He was working with the *Saturday Night Live* comedy show on NBC, and with John Belushi, he developed the Blues Brothers sketch as a preshow warmup for studio audiences. Aykroyd assumed the role of a tall, if not so lean, harmonica player named Elwood Blues; Belushi took the part of a short, mop-haired, roly-poly singer named Jake Blues. Dressed sombrely in black fedoras, black suits and Ray-Ban sunglasses for added comic effect, they performed soul and R&B songs from the 1960s, backed by the *Saturday Night Live* band.

Audiences loved the sketch. It was high-spirited and entertaining, and soon Aykroyd and Belushi began incorporating it into live telecasts. In September 1978, they recorded a concert in Los Angeles for their first album, *Briefcase Full of Blues,* which included three songs from Downchild's *Straight Up* album: "(I Got Everything I Need) Almost," by Donnie Walsh; "Flip, Flop and Fly," by Charles E. Calhoun and Lou Willie Turner; and "Shot Gun Blues," music by Donnie Walsh, lyrics by Richard Walsh. "Here's a song by the Downchild Blues Band called 'Almost,'" Belushi announces to a screaming crowd halfway through the first side.

Briefcase Full of Blues quickly sold more than a million copies, becoming a cult phenomenon that led to a Blues Brothers movie starring Aykroyd and Belushi, which in turn grossed more than $32 million in its first two months in 1980. The soundtrack became their second album. A "best of" record became their third.

Every song they performed proved inferior to its original, both comedians freely admitted, but the Walsh brothers never capitalized on the Blues Brothers' success. They differed over the band's musical direction, with Mr. Downchild wishing to stay with a jumped-up style of blues, and Hock preferring a more rural, rootsier feel. By the time the movie came out, Hock had left for a solo career. The band, except on rare occasions, continues to play and tour without him.

"Belushi and I met for the first time at the Knob Hill Hotel in Scarborough," Hock recalls. "It must have been the late 1970s. Danny brought him down, and I remember Belushi said to me, 'Are you the guy who wrote "Shot Gun Blues"? That's my favorite song.' And I'm thinking, 'John, you're pretty close to the pinnacle of your success here, and you're telling me you're carrying this thing around with you?'"

Anybody whose favorite song is "Shot Gun Blues," Hock means, has to be pretty troubled. "My life is like water swirling down the drain," the song goes. "I'm going to take a shot gun, people, and disconnect my brain."

"I believe John Belushi was an introverted man," Hock continues. "I believe he was a confused man – confused about his own talent and his own apparent value to the world. I got the impression that he was a guy who didn't understand why he had lucked into all this, and that he was living in fear. If you don't understand your own worth, you're living in fear of somebody coming up and saying, 'No, not you, just kidding – you have to give it all back.' It's scary waiting for the artistic police to come and get you. You're not living a lie, but you feel you are. You think, 'One day everybody is going to find out that I have no talent after all,' and you will end up among the artistically homeless.

"I told Belushi," Hock says, "that I thought he was introverted and running scared. But we didn't talk much, probably because I'm the same kind of guy. 'Shot Gun Blues' might have been John Belushi's theme song, but I'm the guy who wrote it."

35

The Horseshoe Tavern

368 QUEEN STREET WEST

The Police played the Horseshoe Tavern on their first North American tour, drawing about 20 people over two nights to shows that thousands of fans now say they saw. "There wouldn't have been room for all the people who have told me personally that they were there," says Gary Cormier, the promoter who booked the band in late 1978. "Almost nobody was there – a handful of people from the record company, and a bunch of regular barflies who were there for everything no matter what it was."

A year earlier, Cormier had formed a partnership with another promoter, Gary Topp, to bring bands to town that they wanted to see themselves and that no established promoter was paying attention to. They called themselves Discreet Consulting, but everybody else called them "the Garys." Working first at the New Yorker Theatre, they began importing hard-edged New York acts such as the Ramones, the Cramps, and Tom Waits. Then they moved to the Horseshoe.

The club stands on the north side of Queen Street near Spadina Avenue, its front door opening to a deep, narrow room with a massive bar along the left side, and beyond it a boxlike cavity with a stage at the back wall. When it opened in 1947, a television offered the primary entertainment. In the 1950s, it became a popular jazz spot. In the late 1960s, it reigned as a country-music hall. In the late 1970s, at the height of the disco craze and when most rock promoters were booking stadium shows, the Garys turned the Horseshoe into a rock club.

"We wanted to get something going," Cormier says. "We got talking with an agent in England about a whole bunch of these weird new British bands – people like XTC, Siouxsie and the Banshees, and Generation X with Billy Idol. He also mentioned a band called the Police. I said, 'Oh, is that the band with Andy Summers, who used to play with Kevin Coyne?' Gary and I were huge fans of this guy from England called Kevin Coyne, a real eccentric singer-songwriter. He had put out a number of records, and on one of them was this guitarist named Andy Summers. The agent said, 'I don't know, I'll check,' and a couple of days later he called back and said, 'Yes, Andy Summers used to play with Kevin Coyne.' So that was the main reason we booked the Police – to talk to Andy about Kevin Coyne."

The Police consisted of Andy Summers on lead guitar, Stewart Copeland on drums, and Sting on bass and vocals. They had come together in mid-1977 as a punk band, but punk crowds had rejected them as too old and too musically advanced. Summers was 35, Sting 26, Copeland 25. All were seasoned musicians who had played with other bands. About the only person who accepted them as hard-edged punkers was an advertising agent for Wrigley's chewing-gum, who hired them for a television commercial on the condition that they change their hair. "You have to be blond," he said.

Dyed-blond hair became their look, and by the time the Garys heard of them, the Police were forging their musical identity as well. With borrowed money they recorded their first single, "Roxanne," which opened with 16 bars of medium-tempo reggae, shifted into eight bars of rock and roll, then slipped back into a reggae shuffle. Pleased with the innovation, they continued to explore blends of reggae, rock, and punk in a way that earned them a place in British "new wave."

The problem was that in England, as in North America, the music industry had grown stale and corporate. New voices could not break through. To get something going from their end, Miles and Ian Copeland, elder brothers to Police drummer Stewart Copeland, decided to introduce British new wave to North America. Working out of London, England, and Atlanta, Georgia, respectively, they established a tour circuit along the New England coast, setting each stop within driving distance of the next and accepting the $200 to $500 a night that a local band would normally charge. A tour could break even, Ian once said, if group members travelled by van with all their equipment and stayed in double rooms at Travelodges.

"The way it worked," Cormier explains, "is that one band would be arriving from England at Kennedy Airport as another band finished the tour. The two would meet in one of the waiting areas. The incoming band would receive the keys and instructions as to where the van was in the parking lot, then get right into it before the engine even had a chance to cool off, and start hot-footing it around the same schedule that the previous band had just completed.

"And as these vans were making their way around the circuit," Cormier continues, "they were also being vandalized in each and every city. You know it's not uncommon for girls to take something off a van as a memento of, say, their first sort of real rock-band experience. So this van literally came into Canada three times with no licence plates. There would be a piece of cardboard with numbers written in gaffer's tape."

The first group to hit the circuit was Squeeze. Ultravox and XTC followed. The Police arrived at JFK on October 20, 1978, via Freddie Laker's Skytrain, the discount air carrier, for a date that night in the Bowery at CBGB. They went on to play clubs in Poughkeepsie, Willimantic, and Swissvale, as well as Boston, Detroit, and – thanks to the Garys – Toronto. Within a year, the Police would sell 2 million albums and 5 million singles worldwide, going on to become one of the most popular groups of the early 1980s for such songs as "Message in a Bottle," "Don't Stand So Close to Me," and "Every Breath You Take." On that first tour, however, the band played 23 shows in 27 days for a gross income before expenses of $7,142. In Poughkeepsie, they played to an audience of three people. "We were pioneering," Summers said at the time. "It was us against the system."

The Police drove into Toronto for dates at the Horseshoe on November 2 and 3, 1978, a Thursday and Friday night.

(Photo courtesy Gary Topp)

"The Garys" bring the Police to town for a return engagement in 1979 as the British new-wave band began to rack up major record sales. Left to right are: Gary Cormier, Sting (vocals), Andy Summer (guitar), Stewart Copeland (drums), and Gary Topp.

On their arrival, Cormier first took them to CHUM-FM, "and we were physically escorted out the door," he says. "CHUM did not want to know about punk bands."

At the club, the audience was minuscule but enthusiastic.

"The band came out and you'd have to be, like, on the planet Zotron not to realize that they were onto something," says Cormier. "Gary and I were doing sound and lights, and within two bars of the first song, we both looked at each other with our mouths open. You knew immediately that something was going to happen with these guys in a major way."

When the last set ended, the three band members headed downstairs to the dressing room, but the tiny audience started screaming for more. People became adamant, prompting Cormier to go down to ask them to come back.

"I walked into the room, and Sting was already undressed," Cormier says. "He went back and played in his underwear."

36

The SkyDome

1 BLUE JAYS WAY

Madonna was sweeping through North America on her 1990 Blond Ambition tour when she stopped at the SkyDome for concerts on three successive nights. Shortly before the third show, on May 29, city police arrived. They said that when the time came for her to sing "Like a Virgin" from a large bed, she must not touch herself in a sexual manner. Members of the public, they said, had been complaining.

No such complaints had reached the press. On the contrary, from the moment Madonna arrived in town, the papers fussed over her every move. The *Sun* ran a picture of her in a track suit, baseball cap and sunglasses, jogging near Casa Loma with her brother and artistic director, Christopher. The *Toronto Star* photographed her leaving Bellini's Italian restaurant, at 101 Yorkville Avenue, on her way back to the nearby Four Seasons Hotel, where she was

Looking more athletic than lewd, Madonna flies through a number during her Blond Ambition tour of 1990. She performed the show as planned even when Toronto police threatened to arrest her if she simulated orgasm.

(Photo: Canapress)

staying. Both papers were running Madonna look-alike contests, and *Toronto Star* social columnist Rita Zekas snagged interviews with an unidentified dentist and his hygienist, summoned to examine a tooth that Madonna had chipped the first night on a microphone.

"We just had a look at it," the dentist said. "It was a very, very small chip and no treatment was necessary."

Opening-night reviews of the show were ecstatic.

"A constantly moving spectacle of dance, design and high-tech eroticism," said the *Toronto Star.*

"Sexy, sassy and just a bit cut-up campy," said the *Sun.*

"A spectacle against which future musical tours can and should be judged," said the *Globe and Mail.*

All mentioned the "Like a Virgin" number. "It began with Madonna rising onto the stage on a red satin bed," wrote Alan Neister in the *Globe and Mail,* "and finished with her thrashing about on the bed in a masturbatory excess."

The critics seemed entertained by the interpretation, but several parents attending with their children apparently were not. Following the first concert, they filed complaints with the police, who responded by dispatching two undercover officers to the second show. On the third night, the officers returned to order Madonna to tone the number down.

Two movie crews working for Madonna filmed the police intervention. One followed the singer as she changed into a pointy gold corset in a room off the main dressing room now used by the Toronto Argonauts football team. The other tracked Madonna's manager, Freddy de Mann, as he intercepted the police at field level and tried to negotiate with them. The spliced footage forms part of Madonna's concert-tour documentary, *Truth or Dare,* now available on home video.

The sequence opens with shots of Madonna's name on the SkyDome marquee, and fans pouring through the gates. The scene then cuts to the dressing room, where Madonna is checking a high-angle ponytail in a mirror, as her brother Christopher nervously tugs at his T-shirt. He tells her that the police have arrived at the stadium and that she will be arrested if she performs "the masturbation scene."

Madonna laughs.

Christopher says he's serious.

"So what's considered masturbation?" she asks.

"When you stick your hand in your crotch," he says.

The film cuts to field level, where Freddy is trying to bluff two grim-faced police officers. He says that if they insist the show be changed, Madonna can always cancel.

The officers, not backing down, agree. And without apparent irony one of them adds, "It's in your hands."

Back in the dressing room, the threat of arrest begins to sink in. An uneasy exchange ensues. Madonna asks what will happen if she goes ahead as planned. What would be the penalty?

The police might stop the show, Christopher says.

The police would take her to the station, an unidentified aide offers. They would write her a ticket, she would have to pay a fine, and the arrest would make newspapers all over the world.

"Yeah!" says Madonna, with a loud clap of her hands. She vows not to change the show.

The film cuts back to Freddy. A crowd of serious-looking men has gathered as negotiations intensify. Freddy tells the police that he wants to talk to a lawyer before making a decision.

Madonna pulls on a jacket with slits for her bra to stick through. She pouts and accuses her brother of lying. He insists this is no joke. The police are downstairs with a representative from the Crown Attorney's office, he says.

Freddy proposes to the police that somebody announce that some scenes might offend some viewers. The police say no – a warning would make no difference.

Showtime nears. Madonna walks into an open area of the dressing room and tells her seven male dancers and two female backup singers that the police are backstage. "What? Why? Are you serious?" everybody says at once. Preshow tensions rise an extra notch. As the performers prepare to leave the room, Madonna gathers everyone into a circle for a ritual preshow prayer.

"Dear Lord," she begins emotionally, her eyes closed and head bowed. "This is our last night in Toronto. The fascist state of fffu-Toronto. And all my little babies are feeling fragile." She tells them that she loves them all, and that she wants everybody to have a great show. "And remember," she says, her voice breaking, "that in the United States of America there is freedom of speech, and, uhhh – let's kick ass."

Freddy appears. Madonna tells him she will not change her show. The two are meeting for the first time since the police arrived, and Freddy begins to brief her on what is happening. Madonna, interrupting, repeats that she will not change her show. She asks him to go back and tell the police of her decision.

Freddy rejoins the officers. The issue, he says, is artistic freedom.

The show is travelling through major cities in several countries, he tells them, and if Canadian authorities arrest Madonna onstage, they risk an international scandal.

Madonna leaves the dressing room. Flanked by backup singers Donna Delory and Niki Harris, she walks hand-in-hand down a wide, concrete corridor towards the arena's north-end stage.

"Cel-e-bra-tion," the women sing in unison. "Come togeth-a, in ev-er-y na-tion." Madonna turns to spit. "Get arrested for that," she says.

The film sequence ends there, but a few minutes later, Madonna took the stage before a thunderous crowd and cried, "Toronto, do you believe in freedom of expression?" She performed the show unchanged, and the next day police denied trying to censor her in the first place.

Speaking to the *Toronto Star,* Sergeant Sergeant Richard Dewhirst said that undercover officers attended the concert in response to complaints, saw nothing wrong, and left. "I can't imagine anyone would go and tell someone to alter something they haven't seen," he said, perhaps unaware that every moment was documented for later worldwide distribution.

37 National Film Board

150 JOHN STREET

City firefighters don't rescue cats from trees any more, but they respond to other types of what they call "miscellaneous alarms." They still release children from locked bathrooms and help old people who have lost their keys break into their own homes. Once, they helped free Annie Lennox from an elevator.

The Scottish pop diva and former lead singer of the Eurythmics arrived in town on March 13, 1995, to launch her second solo album, *Medusa.* That night she appeared live on MuchMusic's *Intimate and Interactive* show, performing before a select studio audience and taking questions from viewers. Partly, she projected the androgynous ice-queen persona of her early videos. She wore a burnt-orange pinstriped suit and purple track shoes – "the only person in the world who could look cool in that," *Toronto Star* reporter Peter Howell said. Partly, she assumed the more relaxed posture of a 40-year-old mother of two young children who was happy to work just part-time. "I don't have any plans to tour," she said affably at one point, as more than 200 people in the street pressed against the exterior glass wall. "But hey, you never know. I may change my mind tomorrow." Backed by three soul singers and a six-piece band, she also belted out seven songs that included "Here Comes the Rain Again" from her Eurythmics days and a rendition of Neil Young's "Don't Let It Bring You Down" from her new album.

Afterwards, Lennox crossed the street to a party. She and her band members, with a throng of handlers and hangers-on, entered the National Film Board building at 150 John Street and stepped onto the elevator to get to the BMG Music offices on the sixth floor. Except too many got on at once.

"I was yelling for some of them to get off," says Jim Campbell, BMG's vice-president of marketing, who stayed off himself. "Then the drummer started jumping up and down, and the elevator started to sink. As it started to sink, the doors closed, and when they closed they would not open again."

Fifteen people were trapped. Campbell called the building superintendent, who called an elevator mechanic, who after half an hour was still nowhere to be found. Campbell then called the fire department, which dispatched four firefighters in three minutes, six seconds. By then, the situation had begun to deteriorate.

"It was getting very hot in the elevator and the fan was not working," the fire captain, Craig Manderson, reported in a document labelled "Miscellaneous Alarms, Incident No. 09436." "The people inside were starting to get very panicky."

At first, Manderson tried to coax the doors open. Then he tried to force them. "We pried the doors open about a foot," the captain reported, "and the people inside seemed to calm down."

A full hour and a half after the doors first shut, a mechanic finally arrived to free everybody. Campbell credits the firefighters, however, for rescuing the party mood.

"After they got the doors partway open, we tried to keep everybody upbeat," he says. "As did Annie. I managed to pass them a bottle of tequila, and Annie led everybody in gospel tunes."

38 Royal Alexandra Theatre

260 KING STREET WEST

Martin Short, Eugene Levy, Dave Thomas, Andrea Martin, Gilda Radner, and Paul Shaffer all got their start together at the Royal Alexandra Theatre in the rock musical *Godspell.* It opened on June 1, 1972.

"We were all 22 years old, and it was our first time in show business, and we became fast friends," Shaffer once recalled. "Danny Aykroyd was around then. He wasn't in the show, but he was a friend of Gilda's. We all hung out extensively. Four of us – Marty, Eugene, Dave, and I – hung out *very* extensively. We used to go over to Marty and Eugene's house Friday nights and just try to make each other laugh."

The Royal Alex is now a national historic site, not because of *Godspell,* but because of the theatre's enduring Edwardian splendor. A plaque to the left of the main door says that the building was constructed in 1907, by a man with the improbable name of Cawthra Mulock. When work began he, too, was 22 years old. He was the city's youngest millionaire, the president of Guardian Trust, Canada Bread, and the National Iron Works. He was also an avid theatre-goer who wished to build "the finest theatre on the continent," he said. To begin he hired an architect trained in elegant Beaux Arts design, and decorators with a taste for velvet and gilt. The acoustics proved excellent, the sightlines superb, and the opulent decor a perfect backdrop to the elaborate formal apparel of theatre-going society.

For years, the Royal Alex prospered as a venue for touring companies based in London and New York. Famous Canadian-born actors also appeared on its stage, including Mary Pickford, Fay Wray, Raymond Massey, and Hume Cronyn. After World War II, however, the building's lustre began to fade. Competition from movies and television increased, and lavish new stage productions were proving too ambitious for a relatively small theatre that seated 1,525 people. In 1962, the apparent death blow came. The more spacious O'Keefe Centre (now the Hummingbird Centre) opened nearby, at Yonge and Front Streets, and the Royal Alex went up for sale. Demolition appeared certain. Then in 1963, a buyer materialized in the unlikely form of Ed Mirvish, proprietor of the gaudy Honest Ed's discount emporium at Bloor and Bathurst Streets.

In a move that has endeared him to the city's cultural community ever since, Mirvish restored not only the theatre, but also the habit of theatre-going among tens of thousands of Torontonians. He sold plays at the Royal Alex the way he sold brooms and stewing pots at Honest Ed's – by offering cut-rate prices. He created the subscription series, or what he called the "package deal," in which customers bought tickets for the same seats at a discount price to a series of short-run shows over one season. He also mounted shows that people wanted to see.

"I'm commercial," he says now of his theatre interests, which have come to include – as a partner with his son, David – the nearby Princess of Wales Theatre and the Old Vic Theatre in London, England. "If you're running a dress department, and you buy only dresses *you* like, you go broke," he says.

His philosophy led him to import two early rock musicals, smash hits that helped ensure the Royal Alex's survival. The first was *Hair,* in 1970, a rambunctious New York hit that featured full frontal nudity and drug-culture radicalism. It ran for 51 weeks, a national record at the time.

The second was *Godspell.* Loosely adapted from the gospel of St. Matthew, it told of Christ's life and teachings through clownlike costumes and high-spirited action. Like *Hair,* it was produced in New York but staged by local performers. Audiences loved it.

A psychedelic drawing of Christ graces an advertisement for the rock musical *Godspell* in 1972. "I've seen it three times and I've become addicted," wrote *Toronto Sun* critic George Anthony.

"Fast and furious, *Godspell* is performed by an exceptionally brilliant cast," *Toronto Sun* critic George Anthony wrote of opening night. "They sing, dance, do impressions … and they earned their three-storey, four-curtain-call, standing ovation that shook the Royal's red-velvet rafters … Andrea Martin's 'Day by Day,' was downright glorious."

A month later, Anthony reviewed the play again.

"I've seen it three times now and I've become addicted," he wrote. "Mr. Short is a gifted mimic. So are Gilda Radner and Eugene Levy, making a fine comedic trio … Seeing them again, witnessing their raw energy and disciplined musical talent, and especially their high professional standards, only makes me hunger for more."

Godspell ran at the Royal Alex for the entire summer. After a one-week hiatus, it reopened with the same cast at the Playhouse Theatre on Bayview Avenue, where it continued for another year. Then a new opportunity arose. Two members of Chicago's Second City comedy troupe, Joe Flaherty and Brian Doyle-Murray, arrived to proselytize their style of improvisational comedy and to open a Second City branch at 110 Lombard Street, near Queen and Jarvis Streets. They raided the *Godspell* crowd. Early recruits included Gilda Radner, Dan Aykroyd, and two other actors who had been with *Godspell* from the beginning, Jayne Eastwood and Gerry Salsberg. Eugene Levy joined in 1974, Dave Thomas and Andrea Martin in 1975, and Martin Short in 1977.

(Photo courtesy of the Royal Alexandra Theatre)

The *Godspell* cast displays their explosive energy on stage at the Royal Alexandra Theatre. Left to right, top row: Eugene Levy, Victor Garber, Martin Short, Gerry Salsberg (seated). Middle row: Jayne Eastwood, Valda Aviks, Andrea Martin, Gilda Radner. Front: Avril Chown. Not shown: Dave Thomas, who joined the show several weeks into the run, and musical conductor Paul Shaffer.

Second City led to the television comedy *SCTV*. Also starring fellow Canadians John Candy, Catherine O'Hara, and Rick Moranis, it became for most of the cast a launching pad to international fame. The show aired first on the Global Television Network in 1976, went into syndication in the United States, and from 1981 until it ended in 1984, also commanded a late-night Friday slot on NBC.

Paul Shaffer, who had been *Godspell*'s musical director, went to New York in 1975 to play piano for *Saturday Night Live* when that show began on NBC. Aykroyd went the same year. Short followed a few years later. Shaffer advanced as leader of the World's Most Dangerous Band on *Late Night with David Letterman* on NBC, then on CBS. On network-television programs and in Hollywood feature movies, *Godspell* and *SCTV* alumni have continued to run into each other ever since.

Photos of the original *Godspell* cast can be seen at Old Ed's Restaurant, a few doors from the theatre, at 276 King Street West. Enter through the front doors; proceed straight ahead past the statuary, stained glass, and Tiffany lamps; descend the stairs, and at the bottom take a sharp right towards the men's washroom. Opposite the washroom door hang the photos – a giant group picture of all the players in their funny costumes, flanked by 14 individual eight-by-tens. All are autographed. All contain greetings and thank-yous to Ed and Anne Mirvish.

The Pretzel Bell

127 SIMCOE STREET

Feeling too shy to speak at a women's-rights meeting in 1971, Rita MacNeil asked if she could stand up and sing instead. She had only ever sung in public once or twice, but the thought of speaking frightened her more. "I knew I would get caught up in the sentences too much," she says, "or I would take too long to get to the point. I thought I could express myself better in song."

MacNeil is now the star of *Rita & Friends,* the hit music variety show aired weekly on CBC television, and the sole program in the country that brings established and emerging rock acts to a mass middle-of-the-road audience. At the time, however, she was an unknown housewife with two young children. Her husband was understanding, she says, but like many women, she had begun to question the conventional roles that society expects of men and women. Then a friend told her about the Toronto Women's Caucus.

"At first I was not interested in going," MacNeil recalls. "Being a shy person, I didn't know what I would get out of it. But my friend said, 'I think you should come,' so I did."

Meetings were held once a week in a room above the Pretzel Bell tavern, since demolished, on Simcoe Street between King and Adelaide. MacNeil remembers travelling there on the King street-car and ascending the stairs to a room crowded with 50 or so women, all of whom struck her as more articulate than she was.

"I was amazed at the speakers," she recalls, "the different women who were talking about all these wonderful issues that were coming to the forefront at the time. It was very stimulating, and I wanted to express myself in some small way. Every time I'd leave I'd think, 'If only I had said this' or 'If only I had said that.' But I had said nothing – as usual. This would play on my mind, so one day I went home and wrote a song. When I went to maybe my fourth meeting, I asked if it would be all right if I sang something that maybe expressed some of the thoughts that I took from the meetings, or some of my feelings. I mean, they didn't normally have people singing there, but being the understanding folks that they were, they said, 'Well sure, Rita.' So I got up in the middle of the group, and heaven knows how I did it, but I did."

She called the song "Need for Restoration," referring to her need to restore her own sense of well-being. "So I found a man in the good old tradition, being conditioned as I was," she sang. "But ... there was unrest and a need for restoration to fill the needs in me." Since then MacNeil has written hundreds of songs, but "Need for Restoration" was the first, and writing it and singing it before a supportive group proved an act of personal liberation.

"It was a breakthrough," she says. "I had always loved singing, but shyness had definitely been a holdback. That experience helped me a lot. And that was also the very beginning of songwriting for me.

Before, I had all these thoughts and hopes in my mind, but they were just snippets – nothing that ever came together in the way of a song. That experience enabled me to get it all together, and after that, if I wanted to say something, that's how I would express it – through my own compositions."

(Photo courtesy SOCAN)

"Shyness had definitely been a holdback," says Rita MacNeil of her late start in the music business as a mother of two young children. Women's-rights meetings in 1971 stirred her to express herself through music.

Encouraged by the women who heard her that day, MacNeil began to perform regularly at public rallies and consciousness-raising sessions. In 1975 she released *Born a Woman,* the first of her more than a dozen albums. She moved to Ottawa briefly, then in 1979 returned to her native Cape Breton, in Nova Scotia, where she began to attract a mainstream pop audience that by the mid-1980s, extended nationwide.

Rita & Friends made its debut in the fall of 1994 from the top floor of the CBC Broadcasting Centre, three blocks south of where MacNeil first sang to the women's caucus. Ratings showed an audience of 1.7 million viewers, making it the most-watched new show in CBC history.

40 Peermusic
Canada Inc.

119 JOHN STREET

"We didn't write a big hit or anything, or I'd probably be living elsewhere now, but we had fun," says Blair Packham, a guitarist, songwriter, and producer who almost wrote a song once with Alanis Morissette. The two met sometime around May or June of 1993. Roughly two years later, she released *Jagged Little Pill,* the album that within another year had sold more than 12 million copies worldwide to become the best-selling album ever by a female solo artist.

Morissette is from Ottawa, but moved to Toronto after high school in 1991, at age 17. The same year, she released *Alanis,* a teenage dance album that sold more than 100,000 copies in Canada and earned her a Juno for most promising female artist. In 1993, she released a second dance recording, *Now Is the Time,* but she was already looking for a new direction. She was making trips to Los Angeles to meet

(Poster design: Patrick Duffy)

Alanis Morissette, calling herself simply Alanis, gets top billing among Songworks members scheduled to perform at the Ultrasound Showbar in 1993. Morissette sang a folk song called "Gone," which she co-wrote with Steve Haflidson.

music-business people and spending most of her Toronto time composing songs with other writers, an activity that eventually drew her to the cozy basement meeting-room at Peermusic Canada Inc. for a series of workshops called Songworks.

Packham was already attending the sessions with his musical partner and life companion, Arlene Bishop. For years he had been a guitarist and vocalist with the Jitters, a local band popular for such songs as "Last of the Red Hot Lovers" and "'Til the Fever Breaks." By 1993 he had begun producing for other people. More recently, he produced and played backup guitar on Bishop's first independent CD, *Pinky*.

"The idea for Songworks," he says, "came from David Baxter and Scott Dibble. David at that time headed up the Toronto office of Peermusic, which is an international music publisher. Scott is a songwriter who had a band called Watertown, and who is now in Hemingway Corner, a sort of Crosby, Stills, and Nash–type trio. David and Scott were talking one night, and they decided that Peermusic had to get more involved in the local scene, and what would be the best way of doing it.

"Scott said something like, 'Wouldn't it be great to actually have a publisher who didn't just reject your songs, who when you sent in a tape wouldn't just go, "No, thank you"? Wouldn't it be ideal to have a publisher who not only gave you tips on how to make your songs better, in their opinion, but also maybe workshopped the songs with other writers?'

"That was the original idea – a workshop where everybody contributes to other people's songs – but it evolved into a situation where we would pair up to write together. Every third Monday or so, this group of people would show up in the basement of Peermusic, a great little hole in the wall. It's a sort of conference room with tables and couches, as well as DAT machines, a good microphone, and a good pair of speakers.

"At the beginning of every meeting, we would sit around and chat for a while, have a beer – it was very much a social event – and then we would get down to listening to the songs written in the previous period. As a rule, every song was greeted warmly, but you could sort of tell which songs were greeted more warmly. Every song was equal, but some were more equal than others. When a song really hit, you really knew it, and that was a great experience.

Hair falling in her eyes, Alanis Morissette performs at Velvet Underground, at 508 Queen Street West, shortly before her meteoric rise to fame in mid-1995. "She's very attractive and very warm and very funny," says Blair Packham, who once almost wrote a song with her.

(Photo: Matthew Kris-MacCormack)

"At some point, we would also pass a hat around with duplicate numbers in it. Everybody would pull out a number and I would say, 'I've got number 7,' and you'd say, 'Oh, I have number 7 as well,' and so you and I would be expected to come back to the next meeting with a song that we had written.

"Arlene and I joined Songworks in the fall of 1992. We'd been to quite a few meetings by the time Alanis showed up, which was in late spring, and I remember sitting across the table from her. She was wearing a summer dress. The full group wasn't there yet so no introductions had gone around, but I noticed her because she has enormous personal magnetism. She's really beautiful in person. I believe they have downplayed the beauty on purpose so she won't be taken as a bimbo, because she's very attractive and very warm and very funny. She laughs really easily – and that's something else she doesn't do a lot of in her public appearances.

"At the beginning we socialized and joked around a bit, and she was paired up with a guy named Steve Haflidson. She and he wrote a song together called 'Gone,' sort of a folk song – more of a folk song than a country song. Steve played guitar, and she sang the lead vocal. At the next meeting, rather than turning on a tape, which is what we usually did, they performed it live – and it was chilling. It really was wonderful. You could just tell that that song was more equal than others. Later we gave a Songworks showcase at Ultrasound Showbar [at 269 Queen Street West, since closed] and she sang that song, 'Gone,' with Steve on acoustic guitar. Again it easily stood out among a bunch of pretty good songs.

"One or two meetings after she started coming, Alanis and I drew each other's number. We tried to write together and, to tell you the truth, we both kept talking. This is certainly a problem with me, but I guess it was with her as well. We talked about all kinds of things. She was spending some time in L.A. at that point, and she talked about living there. I think she was staying at somebody's house, house-sitting or something like that. She also told me about a boyfriend of hers in L.A. that she had broken up with fairly recently. She was kind of broken up about that. But we were just talking – she certainly wasn't confessing or anything. When I first heard 'You Oughta Know,' I thought, 'Oh, that's the guy,' but I don't think so. She had an immediacy that made you feel that you were intimate with her, but when you look back you think, 'No, she probably wasn't any more revealing to me than she would have been to anybody.' But I enjoyed her company.

"I still have the work tape that we made. What you hear is us giggling a lot at the end of every take, and she's singing sort of dummy words, made-up words, just to try to get something going. It's an interesting artifact, but the song itself isn't so good. She was writing with so many other people, I can't help but imagine that she would have been a little scattered. Apparently she wrote with 60 people in Toronto. That's the figure I heard. She wrote with pretty well any of the name songwriters in town – Stan Meissner, Eddie Schwartz, a number of the Peermusic people. She wrote with Arlene and with me, and in both cases we didn't come up with anything. She was all over the place writing with people.

"Despite the fact that we didn't actually finish anything, I had the impression that she has a very good work ethic. She was working very hard, not because of any outside pressure – it was self-imposed. I think if you felt pretty confident that you were going to get a record contract but didn't have the material yet, and you were dreading the moment when some person from the record company was going to say, 'Here's the song you should record,' you'd probably be scrambling to write your own songs. Certainly that's what I would be doing. I'd be writing like mad. Not that recording other people's material is so terrible, but it might be.

"She played me some of the stuff that she had been working on with other writers. She said, 'This is the direction I would like to go in,' but I have to say that whenever I thought of anything, I was sort of influenced by her dance past. That's probably why I didn't hit it, because I kept thinking, 'Well, she's sort of a dance artist.' If I'd known that her album was going to sound the way it did, I could have given her some of Arlene's songs, because some of those songs would have fit beautifully."

BIBLIOGRAPHY

Bockris, Victor. *Keith Richards: The Biography*. New York: Poseidon Press, 1992.

Cohn, Lawrence, ed. *Nothing But the Blues: The Music and the Musicians*. New York: Abbeville Press, 1993.

Dendy, William, and William Kilbourn. *Toronto Observed: Its Architecture, Patrons and History*. Toronto: Oxford University Press Canada, 1986.

Donegan, Rosemary. *Spadina Avenue*. Vancouver: Douglas & McIntyre, 1985.

Einarson, John. *American Woman: The Story of the Guess Who*. Kingston: Quarry Press, 1995.

_____. *Neil Young: Don't Be Denied*. Kingston: Quarry Press, 1992.

Fawcette, Anthony. *John Lennon: One Day at a Time.* New York: Grove Press, 1981.

Fetherling, Doug. *Some Day Soon: Essays on Canadian Songwriters.* Kingston: Quarry Press, 1991.

Goddard, Peter, and Philip Kamin, eds. *Shakin' All Over: The Rock 'n' Roll Years in Canada.* Toronto: McGraw-Hill Ryerson, 1989.

Hawkins, Ronnie, and Peter Goddard. *Ronnie Hawkins: Last of the Good Ol' Boys.* Toronto: Stoddart, 1989.

Helm, Levon, with Stephen Davis. *This Wheel's on Fire: Levon Helm and the Story of the Band.* New York: William Morrow and Company, 1993.

Heatley, Michael. *Neil Young: His Life and Music.* London: Hamlyn, 1994.

Hoskyns, Barney. *Across the Great Divide: The Band and America.* New York: Hyperion, 1993.

Kallmann, Helmut, Gilles Potvin, and Kenneth Winters, eds. *Encyclopedia of Music in Canada.* Toronto: University of Toronto Press, 1992.

Kay, John, and John Einarson. *John Kay: Magic Carpet Ride.* Kingston: Quarry Press, 1994.

McHugh, Patricia. *Toronto Architecture: A City Guide.* Toronto: McClelland and Stewart, 1989.

Melhuish, Martin. *Heart of Gold: 30 Years of Canadian Pop Music.* Toronto: CBC Enterprises, 1983.

Morrell, Brad. *Nirvana and the Sound of Seattle.* New York: Omnibus Press, 1993.

Palmer, Robert. *Rock and Roll: An Unruly History.* New York: Harmony Books, 1995.

Rolling Stone, Editors of. *Neil Young: The* Rolling Stone *Files.* New York: Hyperion, 1994.

Saidman, Sorelle. *Bryan Adams: Everything He Does.* Toronto: Random House, 1993.

Sanchez, Tony. *Up and Down with the Rolling Stones.* New York: W. Morrow, 1979.

Smith, Cathy. *Chasing the Dragon.* Toronto: Key Porter, 1984.

Sutcliffe, Phil, and Hugh Fielder. *The Police: L'Historia Bandido.* London: Proteus, 1981.

Trudeau, Margaret. *Beyond Reason.* New York: Paddington Press, 1979.

Williams, Paul. *Bob Dylan – Performing Artist: The Early Years, 1960–1973.* Novato, CA: Underwood-Miller, 1990.

Yorke, Ritchie. *Axes, Chops and Hot Licks: The Canadian Rock Music Scene.* Edmonton: Hurtig, 1971.

Young, Scott. *Neil and Me.* Toronto: McClelland and Stewart, 1984.

_____ . *A Writer's Life.* Toronto: Doubleday Canada, 1994.

INDEX